THE ORANGE CITADEL

A History of Orangeism in Portadown District

THE ORANGE CITADEL

A History of Orangeism in Portadown District

Researched, Compiled and Written

by

R. David Jones
James S. Kane
Robert Wallace
Douglas Sloan
Brian Courtney

Published in 1996 by
Portadown Cultural Heritage Committee.

© Portadown Loyal Orange Lodge District No. 1, 1996

ISBN 0 9527111 0 9

Printed by
Trimprint Ltd.,
36 English Street,
Armagh BT61 9BE

Front cover photograph:
The Twelfth of July in Portadown (1928),
Sir John Lavery (1856–1941).
Reproduced with the kind permission
of the Trustees of the Ulster Museum.

Back cover:
The statue of Colonel Saunderson standing
before St Mark's Church of Ireland in Portadown

Contents

Acknowledgements ....*vii*

Foreword .... *viii*

I   Portadown District – The Early Years 1

II   The United Irishmen – The Orange Response 8

III The Period of Consolidation 12

IV The Years of Crisis 15

V   The Right To March 19

VI The Home Rule Crises 26

VII The World Wars 33

VIII The Post-War Era 41

IX The Re-Routing Controversy of 1985 46

X   The Crisis Deepens in 1986 51

XI Portadown District in the 1990s 57

XII The Siege of Drumcree 62

XIII Profiles of District Masters of the Twentieth Century 71

XIV Carleton Street Orange Hall 76

XV Histories of Private Lodges 82

XVI The Orange Trail – A Guide for Visitors and Tourists 102

      Appendix 1 ~ District Masters of Portadown District 105

      Appendix 2 ~ Twelfth of July Venues Since 1870 106

      Footnotes 108

      Bibliography and Sources 110

Acknowledgements

A work of this nature requires the assistance and support of many individuals and organisations. The Cultural Heritage Committee would like to acknowledge the following for their help in the publication of this book:

Portadown District LOL 1

W. Bro. Harold Gracey, Worshipful District Master; Bro. Stanley Thompson, District Treasurer; and all the officers of Portadown District. Bro. Gareth Watson, Treasurer of the Cultural Heritage Committee; Secretaries and members of the private lodges within Portadown District who supplied information or returned the lodge questionnaires. Bro. Douglas Sloan for proofreading the manuscript and for his helpful hints, suggestions and advice.

The Ulster Society

A special word of thanks must go to all at the Ulster Society for the Promotion of Ulster-British Heritage and Culture for all their assistance especially David Bushe who designed the cover and prepared the photographs. Elaine McClure, in a private capacity gave helpful and valuable assistance in preparing the manuscript for publication.

Museums, Libraries and Government Departments

To Mrs Jacqueline Donnelly of County Meath and the Trustees of the Ulster Museum for kind permission to use *12th July Portadown 1928* by Sir John Lavery as the cover of the book.

The Trustees of Armagh County Museum for kind permission to quote from the William Blacker Daybooks.

To the Deputy Keeper of the Public Record Office of Northern Ireland for kind permission to quote from documents held at PRONI.

The staff at the Irish History Section of SELB Headquarters in Armagh for assistance in obtaining copies of old newspapers.

Grand Orange Lodge of Ireland

Bro. George Patton for assisting with information on the early origins of lodges and for allowing access to the GOLI Registers and Minute Books.

Photographs

Bro. Albert Nicholl, *Portadown Times*, and to those too numerous to mention who loaned photographs for inclusion in the book.

The Late Bro. W. H. Wolsey

Finally, the members of the Cultural Heritage Committee would like to put on record the great debt of gratitude that we all owe to the late Bro. W. H. Wolsey, the author of *Orangeism in Portadown District*, published in 1935. Due to the meticulous research of W. H. Wolsey the history of Orangeism in the area is perhaps the most comprehensive of any District within the jurisdiction of the Grand Orange Lodge of Ireland.

Although published in a similar format to Wolsey's accomplished work, this book is offered as a completely new appreciation of Orangeism in the Portadown area, drawing as it does material from a wide variety of new sources. The sixty years since the appearance of Wolsey's book is dealt with in considerable detail, bringing the story right up to date. It is our hope that in the years to come *The Orange Citadel* will rank alongside its illustrious and now rather scarce predecessor.

History is of course an ongoing process and so the authors of this work would respectfully request that in the years ahead future generations of Orangemen will continue to update the History of Orangeism in Portadown District. The story continues...

Foreword

1996 is a momentous year for the Orange brethren of Portadown as it marks the bicentenary of the formation of Portadown District LOL 1.

While the seeds of Orangeism were sown at the Diamond and Loughgall in 1795, the formation of the first District Lodge at Portadown on 21 August 1796 was to set in motion the organisational structure of the Institution that would prosper within the County of the Diamond, the country and throughout the world.

The intervening years have seen many members from lodges within Portadown District serve their country and their town with distinction at all levels. Outstanding service has been given by Orange brethren during the growth and development of the town of Portadown in areas such as local government, health, education and commerce.

I would like to thank and congratulate those members of the Cultural Heritage Committee of Portadown District Lodge who have given freely of their time to painstakingly research and document the information contained in this book. Each individual Orangeman in the District owes them a debt of gratitude.

I would commend this history to members of the Order of all ages, both in Portadown and further afield, to be read so that they might further their knowledge of the origins of the Institution to which they have the privilege to belong.

For those who may not be members of our Order I would suggest a reading of this history may assist them to gain a more broadly based understanding of Orangeism and Orange Culture which may in turn dispel some of their previously held misconceptions and misunderstandings.

Harold Gracey
Worshipful District Master
Portadown District LOL 1

I

Portadown District – The Early Years

The Williamite Legacy

THE Williamite era bequeathed a deep legacy to the Protestant people of Ireland; the memory of victorious deliverance from sectarian threat and a strong sense of communal identity, centred around a popular hero figure in the person of King William III. Indeed a small number of men from around the Portadown area had taken part in the fighting at the Battle of the Boyne and had earlier endured the terrible conditions at the siege of Londonderry. One of those present was Captain William Blacker – an ancestor of the celebrated Lt.-Col. William Blacker, who will feature prominently in the story of Orangeism in Portadown District.

Although King William himself never stayed in or passed through Portadown on his way to the Boyne, elements of his army, under the command of Field Marshal Schomberg, certainly made their presence felt in the area. Just prior to the Battle of the Boyne one Paul le Harpur, cider-maker to the Prince of Orange, arrived in Portadown with the necessary equipment for producing cider for the Williamite army. A Welsh regiment was stationed for a time in the townland of Ballyworkan being billeted in the vicinity of where Pepper's Trees now stand and in the townland of Drumnacanvy is the site of Schomberg's Tower. It is also interesting to note that in the vicinity of where the Ulster Bank is now, stood King William's pear tree, further evidence of the presence of Orange forces in 1689–90.

Captain William Blacker served with distinction throughout the Williamite campaign during the siege of Derry, the Battle of the Boyne and at the siege of Limerick. In later years folk memories of this service would be kindled by the family's possession of the gloves and saddlecloth used by King William III at the Battle of the Boyne.

These items had come into the possession of Colonel Carey, the grand uncle of Lt.-Col. William Blacker, who presented them to his nephew at an Orange parade in 1797. For many years these items remained in the possession of the Blacker family who presented them to Portadown District LOL No. 1, which in turn loaned them to the Portadown Museum. The saddlecloth and gloves are now in the safekeeping of the Grand Orange Lodge of Ireland and are on display at the House of Orange in Belfast.

Celebrations of these victories at Londonderry, the Boyne and Aughrim long predated the eventual emergence of the Orange Order in 1795. Some officers, who were veterans of the Williamite campaigns in Ireland, formed themselves into a type of Regimental Association known as the Knights of the Boyne. Captain William Blacker was a member and there is a painting, surmounted by the insignia of the Order, of him complete with period costume. Almost 100 years later his descendant and namesake Lt.-Col. William Blacker became involved with a group known as the 'Loyalty Lads' whilst still a pupil of Armagh Royal School. This group was formed in the early 1790s and even before the Orange Order was formed, took the colour orange, in the form of ribbons, as their badge of recognition.

However, the folklore and the memory of past victories was not just confined to the ruling classes; it also remained amongst the farmers, labourers and estate workers as well as artisans and tradesmen. Stories were told and handed down from generation to generation, and during the agrarian conflict that erupted in North Armagh during the late 18th Century, the Protestants of the area evoked the memory of the 'Great Deliverer' as a rallying cry to their cause.

William Blacker wrote of one man in particular who had known people from the

Portadown area who had taken part in the Battles of the Boyne and Aughrim. His name was William Lutton, who lived on the Carrickblacker estate. In the words of Blacker, Lutton '...was born in 1710, only 20 years after the Battle of the Boyne so that at 20 must have met and conversed with many who had been stout young fellows from 25 to 30 in that memorable action...'[1]

As Lutton recounted the stories and anecdotes of old, similar men of resolute character, themselves descendants of those who had fought with King William at the Boyne, were preparing to defend their homes against the forces of evil and tyranny. This action, now known to history as the Battle of the Diamond, was on a much smaller scale and those involved were part of no regularly constituted army. However the 'Diamond Fight' which ultimately gave rise to the Orange Order, would be no less significant to the Protestants of Ireland, when compared to the mighty clash of kings at the River Boyne in 1690.

The Battle of the Diamond

For many years prior to 1795 there had been attacks on the Protestants of Armagh by various secretive and violent organisations. William Blacker recorded that as early as 1759 one such group, known as the White Boys Association was in existence. This organisation later became the Defenders, a group which terrorised isolated settlements of Protestants throughout County Armagh. In 1783 the Defenders attempted to prevent the celebration of 12 July at Lisnagade Fort near Scarva. Later, attacks on Protestants became so commonplace, that few dared travel alone, particularly at night. In one notably savage incident the Forkhill home of a schoolmaster, named Barclay, was attacked and he, his wife and her teenage brother had their tongues cut out.

By 1795 the Defenders had become so bold that a force of 300 openly attacked a 20-strong detachment of the Clare Militia, who were transporting ammunition from Armagh to Tandragee, in broad daylight. This attack was beaten off, but it was only a prelude to what was to come. The Defenders had set their sights on the strategic little

hamlet of the Diamond, midway between Portadown and Loughgall. Alerted to the Defenders' plans, Protestants rallied from several areas – Loughgall, Richhill, the Dyan and Portadown – to resist the impending assault. William Blacker spent many hours in the company of a carpenter called Macan, making ammunition from the lead on Carrickblacker House from where he conveyed it to the Diamond.

The victory at the Diamond was not in itself any more significant than earlier defeats of Defender attacks. The significance of the Diamond lay in what followed the battle, namely the birth of the Orange Institution. Following the rout of the Defenders the victorious Protestants agreed on the need for a defensive organisation. Over a period of two centuries this has grown to the point where some claim that the Orange Institution was formed outside the smouldering remains of Dan Winter's cottage in the space of a few hours! This would of course have been impossible. Given the complexity of the organisation that eventually emerged, it is more plausible to suggest that on that night the formation of an association was agreed upon and the detail of the association's creation was passed to those who would be regarded as the natural leaders. Both the Colonel Wallace and William Blacker papers support this interpretation. Blacker noted:

> Immediately after the battle and on the field of action measures were adopted for the formation of a defensive association of Protestants, and these were carried into effect as far as commencement in the house of James Sloan, in the village of Loughgall, about three miles from the Diamond. Sloan acted as Secretary and issued what were called 'numbers', a kind of rude warrant for holding lodges.[2]

The Issue of Warrants

It appears probable that the first few warrants issued were actually promises of warrants to be granted later if the Institution became established on a regular basis. This theory, goes some way towards accounting for the apparent inconsistencies in the issue of various warrant numbers. This in turn led to many colourful stories, legends and folklore surrounding the issue of some warrants. Portadown featured prominently in the issue of what William Blacker termed 'numbers'.

Number 7 was given to Thomas Lecky of Breagh. He was a man of resolute character; a leader at the Battle of the Diamond; and among the first to undertake dangerous enterprises – what these were, we are not informed. However, there is an anecdote regarding the issue of No. 7. The tradition is that Lecky arrived at James Sloan's house in Loughgall when No. 7 was about to be made out to another person, whereupon Lecky flourished a large blackthorn stick threatening to disperse the meeting if he did not receive the number. For the sake of peace, those gathered at Sloan's house, agreed that he should get No. 7. Warrant No. 8 passed to Richard Robinson of Timakeel, whilst No. 9 was issued to a man in the neighbourhood of Portadown, whose name has been lost to history. Warrant No. 10 became the property of George Templeton, one of the three who stormed Faughart Fort. George Innis, an innkeeper in Grange O'Neiland, not far from the Diamond, received Warrant No. 35, whilst No. 40 went to Robert Ruddock.

Defensive Associations

At the same time as the first steps were being taken in the establishment of the Orange Order the inhabitants of several townlands followed the example of the tenants of the Blacker estate near Portadown. They met on 29 February 1796 to consider the issue of threats that had been posted up in the locality. Those present at the meeting unanimously pledged to prevent, if possible, illegal meetings, testify against all lawbreakers regardless of religion and sympathised with a few Roman Catholic neighbours, whose homes had been attacked by the Protestant Peep O' Day Boys. Similar associations were also formed by the Protestants of Drumcree and of Seagoe and although they did not function for long, they inevitably assisted in the spread of the Orange Institution throughout the Portadown area.

The Orange Order is Organised

If the initial response to the proposed establishment of a 'union among Protestants' was favourable there remained the question of deciding on the forms of ritual and ceremony. Those engaged in the initial discussions agreed to meet in Portadown to further investigate this question when they had each concluded business in the market. There, by chance, they encountered George Templeton, holder of warrant No. 10. Templeton, an active Freemason, invited the group into a room where a Masonic Lodge met and in which some Masonic emblems remained on show. James Sloan of Loughgall and James Wilson of the Dyan were also Freemasons so it was inevitable that some Masonic rituals and symbols would be incorporated into the Orange Institution. Historically the town of Portadown stands out as the place where the first, albeit crude, form of Orange ritual was decided upon.

There were also other influences, apart from Freemasonry, on the embryonic Orange Order, the most important of which was the influence of the military. The military link was forged at a very early stage when three officers namely Captain Gifford, Colonel Sheldrake and Captain Cramp, all of whom had been dispatched to Loughgall, following the Battle of the Diamond, actually joined the Orange Order. They attended at least one meeting of the nascent body and 'assisted in organising the system, to which they took kindly'.[3] In later years military figures such as Colonel William Verner and Lt.-Col. William Blacker would carry on this close association.

The Landed Gentry Become Involved

In the rigidly structured society of the late eighteenth century the survival and growth of the proposed Orange Order depended heavily on the attraction of, and guidance by, members of the landed gentry. These men possessed the education, resources and expertise required to shape and develop the body. They also wielded considerable influence, by virtue of their position in society, with the authorities and this in turn helped those in power to tolerate the growth of the Orange Institution. Finally they had considerable power to influence and encourage the tenants on their estates to follow in their footsteps and join the Orange Order.

The first member of the landed gentry to become a member of the Orange Institution was William Blacker, who obtained warrant No. 12 for himself and the workers on his father's estate at Carrickblacker. In his subsequent memoirs, Blacker recorded that 'very few of the resident gentry of the County joined in the first instance. Of these few were my old friend, Joseph Atkinson, Esq.; ...the Rev. George Maunsil, of Drumcree, afterwards Dean of Leighlin; Captain Clarke, of Summer Island, and soon after the young Verners of Church Hill.'[4]

It was, perhaps beneficial to the Institution that in the early initial period, participation by the social elite was confined to a small circle of personal friends such as the men described previously. This may well have prevented any personal rivalries from hampering the development of the Institution. Indeed personal links were significant from the outset of the foundation of the Orange Order. Mr. James Sloan, who in the initial phase acted as secretary and Mr. Wolsey Atkinson of Portadown who carried out the duties of treasurer, were brothers-in-law.

The Importance of Portadown

As the new organisation took shape, with Portadown closely involved in its development, so the spread of the new organisation and its format rested largely on Portadown and its commercial and communication links. The completion of the Newry Canal in 1742 ,was both a cause and consequence of eighteenth century prosperity in Ulster...'[5] and a major foundation in the growth of Portadown until the 20th Century. The Linen Industry was the boom sector in the economy of the time with its heart being the 'Linen Triangle extending from Dungannon east to Lisburn and south to Armagh'.[6] Portadown, one of about fifty market towns with a population of 500 or more, stood at the centre of this triangle.

For most people in Ulster the roads remained as the principal means of communication and one of 'the two most important turnpike roads ran from Armagh to Lis-

burn...'.[7] Lt.-Col. William Blacker also referred to this vital factor: 'The great roads leading from Tandragee to Lurgan and from Banbridge to Portadown after meeting and crossing each other at Drumlin Hill run parallel for the distance of about a mile. They are connected near the gate of Carrick by a narrow road called the Long Lonan...'[8] The connection between trade, communication and ideas is a well established truism of history. For the growth of the Orange Order it was indeed fortunate that its inception lay close to Portadown with its road and water routes to hand.

The First Orange Demonstration – 12 July 1796

Only ten months after the historic Battle of the Diamond the Orangemen of County Armagh met to openly celebrate for the first time. In a letter, written on 13 July 1796, to Lord Camden, Lord Gosford wrote of a first hand account of an Orange procession which he witnessed in his demesne:

> My Lord I have the honour to acquaint Your Excellency that the meeting of the Orangemen took place yesterday in different parts of this County; one party consisting of 30 companies with banners, flags etc; after parading through Portadown Loughgall and Rich-Hill came towards this place... They accordingly came here about five o'clock in the evening marching in regular files by two and two with orange cockades unarmed, and by companies which were distinguished by numbers upon their flags. The devices on the flags were chiefly portraits of King William with mottoes alluding to his establishment of the Protestant religion, and on the reverse side of some of them I perceived a portrait of his present Majesty with the crown placed before him, motto God Save The King... The number who paraded through my place amounted I should imagine to about 1500.[9]

This is a remarkable and very revealing eyewitness account of what was the first ever Orange demonstration to take place in County Armagh. What Lord Gosford termed companies (probably due to their military countenance on parade), were of course Orange lodges. The peer also describes how each company carried a flag or banner with a number which obviously corresponds to the warrant number of each particular lodge.

As yet the style of regalia had not been decided upon, nor had as yet evolved into a uniform pattern. Whilst some members wore orange ribbons, cockades (as reported by Lord Gosford) or sashes, many wore no recognisable symbols whatsoever. William Blacker, who was then a student at Trinity College, Dublin, later noted that there were about ninety active Orange lodges in the country around this time.

Whilst the public demonstration was under way, Portadown was the venue for a representative meeting, held to address the question of establishing a governing body or Grand Lodge to oversee the administration of the flourishing Orange movement. Again following the pattern of the post-Diamond period, it was decided to adjourn to permit the various lodges to consider and report back. In the meantime members of the various lodges in the Portadown area met to consider the setting up of their own body which would act as an umbrella organisation for the lodges in and around Portadown.

The Formation of Portadown District
Portadown was, as ever, to the forefront in adopting the new Orange organisation and the influential members of the various lodges felt that the time was now right to establish a new District Lodge. There is some debate as to who was responsible for this far reaching move and indeed who had the honour of being elected as the first District Master of Portadown. The Colonel Wallace papers name Daniel Bulla as having been granted promissory (warrant) Number 89 on 7 July 1796 and describe him as District Master of Portadown. W. H. Wolsey, however, names John Burleigh of Burleigh House, Meadow Lane, as having been the first District Master from the District's inception on 21 August 1796 to 1807. Whatever the reason for this discrepancy there is no doubt as to when Portadown Orange District came into formal being. The date was 21 August 1796 and Portadown

has the unrivalled distinction of forming the first District Orange Lodge in the history of the Institution.

Portadown District comprised 23 private 'numbers' or lodges as follows: 7, 8, 9, 10, 13, 18, 19, 20, 25, 31, 35, 40, 56, 58, 78, 80, 89, 99, 107, 172, 174, 318, and 417. Four more lodges namely 516, 755, 831 and 948 were added a year later. It can obviously be seen that almost all the lodges mentioned are still in existence in Portadown, although they may not all be in the areas in which they were formed. There have of course been other changes to these numbers in the intervening years.

The regulations by which the District organised and ran itself are the earliest set of rules for an Orange District and because of their historic importance are set out in full as follows:

Rules of Portadown Orange District, 21 August 1796

1 ~ That there is a committee of the whole of the Masters of the District authorised to hold a meeting once every three months at the house of Abraham Dawson in Portadown in order to transact any business relative to this District.

2 ~ That if any member of any lodges of this District be censured and found guilty by the body he belongs to, if he thinks himself aggrieved he has a power to appeal to the above committee for redress, and whatever they conclude on is hereby deemed final.

3 ~ That any Master absenting himself from our quarterly meeting and not deputing a man to act in his place, is to be fined in two shillings eight and a half pence for each offence and also that no Master is to leave the room of the meeting without leave from the Chair or be fined for each offence in six and a half pence.

4 ~ That any member withdrawing a certificate from the body he belongs he is to pay one shilling one penny for it, said sum to go to the benefit of the body he belongs.

5 ~ That no man whatever who has ever sworn secrecy to United Irishman rules can be admitted as a member amongst Orangemen afterwards unless he prosecutes to conviction the man who administered said trea-

sonable oath and then to be admitted according to the Master of the body's pleasure to which he belongs or to which he applies to become a member.

6 ~ That we appoint James Dawson as our secretary for this committee and he is to observe that if any Master is guilty of cursing an oath while present to have him fined for each offence in sixpence.

7 ~ That any Master of this District who is summoned on twenty-four hours' notice to attend an Orangeman's funeral in this District and does not attend with whatever number of his members he can he is to be fined in five shillings said sum to be paid at our next District meeting.

8 ~ That no Master or member whatever belonging to any Society of the District shall be aiding or assisting in any clandestine manner in making any man an Orangeman.

9 ~ That we will not admit into any Society of the District as a member any stranger until first he produces a certificate of his good character from the Master of the Orange Lodge residing most convenient to where he came from.

10 ~ That any member of any Society of this District who absents himself for three months together from his lodge he is to be summoned in the fourth night to clear off his dues (if any remains) to the body. If he does not attend on that night he is to be tried by the committee of the body and if excluded to be reported to this committee at the next meeting after.

11 ~ That any Master or member of any lodge of this District who will be found guilty of such crime as shall entirely exclude him from the Society, his name and offence shall be published in the Belfast News-Letter.

12 ~ That every member belonging to every lodge of this District will take the proper qualification oath specified in the Dublin resolutions otherwise to be expelled from the lodge they belong to. (Added after 1798)[10]

Due to their importance to Portadown Orangemen these rules are worthy of some study and explanation. The rules first of all indicate that the members of the District regarded that body as a superior lodge, their loyalty being primarily to the Portadown area, rather than to their own private lodges. Great emphasis was put on the character of applicants or visitors, with great care being taken to exclude any person whose loyalty or conduct was doubtful. It must be remembered that the Defender organisation was still very much in evidence and there was also a mention of the rise of the United Irishmen's Society in Rule 5. The Portadown brethren were determined not to allow any person with sympathies towards these groups to become a member, for obvious reasons, of the District. In Rule 11 there was provision for the expulsion of any member convicted of any sufficiently serious crime. Rule 7 makes an interesting comment on the prevailing attitudes of the time. Western European death rates in the late 18th century remained appallingly high. Death was a much more commonplace event than today, and funeral rites, with their attendant display of respect for the deceased and bereaved, were considered an obligation on all classes and creeds.

The Formation of a Grand Lodge at Portadown

By 12 July 1797 the various lodges and districts throughout the country had made their views known regarding the formation of an umbrella organisation to oversee the workings of the Order. Another meeting was held in Portadown to discuss the matter. It was at this meeting that the historic decision was taken to form a Grand Lodge. The structure of this prototype Grand Lodge was a simple bringing together of the Masters and secretaries of the Counties in which the Institution was established. Among those present were: William Blacker, Grand Master of Armagh; Thomas Seaver, Grand Treasurer of Armagh; William Atkinson, Grand Master of Antrim; Thomas Verner, Grand Master of Counties Tyrone, Londonderry and Fermanagh; David Verner, Grand Secretary of Armagh and Wolsey Atkinson, Acting Grand Secretary.[11]

The primacy of County Armagh may be inferred from the presence of Thomas Seaver Grand Treasurer of Armagh and the only treasurer listed. The significant role of Portadown in the development of the Institution can be seen by the position of Wolsey Atkinson as Acting Grand Secretary. William Blacker, also of Portadown, had the honour of being the first Grand Master of Armagh. Thomas Verner and David Verner from Church Hill, County Armagh, were also very much to the fore in the establishment of the Grand Lodge.

Two important resolutions passed at the Portadown meeting, which reflected the hierarchical authority and discipline of this new body were as follows:

1 ~ That all Lodges shall pay an annual sum of three pence for each member, to defray the various expenses incurred by Mr. Atkinson in the issuing of warrants.
2 ~ That no Lodge shall be held without a Warrant, to be signed by Mr. Wolsey Atkinson, and a seal with the likeness of King William affixed thereto.[12]

The formation of a Grand Lodge was a bold step and as a matter of right Loughgall and County Armagh had the honour of being the first seat of the embryonic Orange authority. Colonel Wallace put it succinctly when he wrote 'In the County of the Diamond was formed the premier Grand Lodge; and the first Grand Master was Captain, afterwards Colonel Blacker, of Carrickblacker, the only gentleman of property at the Battle of the Diamond'.[13]

Again, as in the previous year, whilst the leaders of the Order were meeting in Portadown, large public demonstrations were held across Ulster. The Orangemen of Armagh, to the number of 20,000, assembled in the Demesne of Brownlow House in Lur-

gan where they were reviewed by General Knox and General Lake, the Commander in Chief of the Northern District of the British Army. Both men were anxious to see at first hand the discipline and strength of the Orange movement as the government realised that in the event of a rising the military authorities would be in need of such men. Lake and Knox were delighted with what they saw and congratulated William Blacker on the turnout of the men. William Blacker has left us a fascinating account of these celebrations:

From sunrise that morning the whole country was in motion. The people from this quarter first moved to Portadown, where they met those of the districts west of the Bann and proceeded together from thence to Lurgan. Some time before this my grand old uncle, Colonel Carey, had made me a present of an original painting of King William III by Nellor and also of the horse furniture used by that prince at the Battle of the Boyne.[14]

As the year of 1797 drew to a close the Orange movement in Portadown was in a healthy and vibrant state. The brethren there had hosted some of the most important and historic meetings of the embryonic Orange Order and had helped shape and influence its organisation not only in Armagh but throughout the whole country. The year of 1798, the so-called 'Year of Liberty', would see the Orange movement play a significant part in the defeat of the United Irishmen's Rebellion.

II

The Orange Response to the 1798 Rebellion

The Formation of Grand Lodge

ON 8 March 1798 representatives of various Orange Districts and lodges met in Dublin to plan the future organisation of the Orange Order. Amongst those present, which included a large proportion of military officers and NCOs, was the redoubtable Orange leader from Portadown, William Blacker of Carrickblacker. A further two representatives from lodges in Armagh, both military ones from the Armagh Militia, were also in attendance. The basis of the operation of Grand Lodge and the organisational structure of the Order as a whole, which reflected that already adopted by Portadown and County Armagh, were contained in the unanimous resolutions agreed:

Resolved:

That it is highly advisable that a proper correspondence should be forthwith instituted between the different Orange Lodges in this kingdom.

That it is advisable that a Grand Lodge should be formed for that purpose to be held in Dublin.

That this Lodge be called the Grand Lodge of Ireland, for correspondence and information.

For the purpose of carrying the above resolution into effect, that each County should be divided into Districts by the Grand Master and the other Master of the County.

That each District should have a District Master, to be chosen by the Masters of the Lodge in each District.

That each County should have a Grand County Lodge, to be formed of the District Masters.

That it is advisable that the Grand Lodge of Ireland should be formed by members, to be chosen by ballot by each County Grand Lodge, and that the Grand Masters of Counties, District Masters, and the Masters of Lodges in Dublin, on account of their residence, should be members, and that all Masters of County Lodges should be admitted as honorary members, and that each regiment, having one or more members, should have a power of choosing one member by ballot, to be a member of the said Grand Lodge.

That the said Grand Lodge, when formed, should forthwith choose a Grand Master, to be called Grand Master of Ireland.

That the Masters of Lodges, District Masters, Grand Masters of Counties, the Grand Lodge of Ireland, and the Grand Master of Ireland should be re-elected once in every year, one month previous to the first of July (O.S.)

That it is highly advisable that each Master of a Lodge should return the Number of his Lodge, together with the numbers that compose it, to the District Masters, to be returned by them to the Grand Master of the County, and to be laid by him before the Grand Lodge of Ireland.

That it is advisable that the first meeting of the Grand Lodge of Ireland should be on Monday, the 9th April 1798, to be held at the house of Thomas Verner, of Dawson Street Esq. Grand Master of the Counties of Londonderry, Tyrone and Fermanagh.

That a copy of these Resolutions shall be sent to every Lodge in Ireland.

Thomas Verner, Chairman, Master Lodge No. 176, and Grand Master of the Counties of Tyrone, Londonderry and Fermanagh[1]

That first meeting of the restructured Grand Lodge of Ireland was indeed held on 9 April 1798 at the Dawson Street residence of Thomas Verner, a member of the influential Verner family of Church Hill, County

Armagh. Wolsey Atkinson of Portadown, attended as Grand Secretary. Due to the historic origins of the Orange Order and the pride of place that went to County Armagh and also because of the presence of Wolsey Atkinson, those present agreed to grant Armagh the continuing privilege of issuing warrants. In fact no lodge could be held without a warrant signed by Wolsey Atkinson of Portadown and bearing a seal showing King William III, Prince of Orange.

This honour exercised by a resident of Portadown and the need to issue standardised warrants to lodges already in existence, led Colonel Wallace to conclude that 'Portadown soon assumed the ascendancy. The Bann and its historic bridge were there; Mr. William Blacker was there; and there, too, were the manly fellows at whose head he marched to the Diamond.'[2]

The establishment of the Orange Order in Dublin, then the administrative and legislative capital of Ireland, assisted in the Order's growth as it began to attract members of the landed gentry, military officers and other members of the establishment.

The setting up of the Grand Lodge of Ireland coincided with the increasing rise and influence of the United Irishmen's movement which had been founded by Wolfe Tone in 1791. Within a matter of weeks of the formation of the Grand Lodge of Ireland, thousands of members of the Orange Order, including many of the highest ranking officials, would play a major role in putting down the revolt by Tone and his United Irishmen.

The Rebellion Begins
The United Irishmen's Rebellion began in Wicklow, Kildare, Carlow and Meath with attacks on the military garrisons, off-duty members of the yeomanry and the homes of many Protestants. From the outset, however, the rising had been severely weakened by the arrest of many of the leaders of the rebels including Captain Quigley, who had led the Defenders at the Battle of the Diamond, some three years earlier. It was, however, in County Wexford that some of the most atrocious crimes ever to take place in the island of Ireland were committed. The Wexford insurgents were led by Father

John Murphy and were comprised almost exclusively of Roman Catholic peasants. Their subsequent actions bore no relation to the aims of the United Irishmen on whose behalf they were supposedly fighting. They carried out a systematic pogrom against Protestants and loyal Roman Catholic families whose fathers or sons were serving in the militia.

The first major atrocity was enacted at Wexford town where 100 Protestant inhabitants were thrown into the River Slaney in scenes reminiscent of the 1641 massacre at the Bann Bridge in Portadown. At the rebel encampment at Vinegar Hill 200 Protestant men, women and children were murdered. The worst atrocity of the whole campaign, however, occurred at Scullabogue barn where 230 Protestants and Roman Catholics were brutally herded into a barn which was then set alight by the rebels. Only one man survived this terrible ordeal. To the Protestants in the south the peasant revolt was like 1641 all over again, only this time help was at hand in the form of the yeomanry and Orange volunteers.

Armagh Remains Peaceful
In direct response to the rise of the United Irishmen and the all too real threat, at that time, of French Invasion, the authorities began to raise a corps of yeomanry in 1796. It fell to the landed gentry of the country to raise and command these units and to bring them to a state of operational readiness. From the outset the yeomanry in the North was dominated by Orangemen who by virtue of their station in society, either raised the corps or served in the ranks. As many as 15,000 Orangemen served in the yeomanry and many more Orange volunteers helped quell the United Irishmen's rebellion of 1798.

Many yeomanry units were by 1798, Orange lodges, in military uniform, known to be as such by friend and opponent alike. News of the rebellion in the south had already made its way up north and the units waited for the anticipated rising that was to take place on their own soil. The seventh of June saw the beginning of the United Irishmen's revolt in the north but there was to be no repeat of the sectarian slaughter that characterised the rebellion in the southern counties. Many of the insurgents were Presbyterians and as such the rebellion was largely confined to Counties Antrim and Down, however, the presence of so many Orangemen in the historic County of the Diamond was also a major factor in the containment of the rebellion to these counties.

On 10 June Major-General Goldie ordered Captain Atkinson of the Crow Hill Yeomanry to join with the Yeomanry Corps of Portadown and to assist them in holding the pass between Portadown and Lough Neagh. Colonel Wallace declared that 'the peace of Armagh was maintained by the Orangemen',[3] whilst Bardon notes 'such Protestants could congratulate themselves for one of the most striking features of the 1798 Rebellion – the complete failure of mid-Ulster, the home of Defenderism, to take part in the rising.'[4]

Let us now examine the activities, during the 1798 Rebellion, of one of the most well-known yeomanry units in the Portadown area, namely the Seagoe Yeomanry, which consisted largely, though not exclusively, of Orangemen.

The Seagoe Yeomanry

In Portadown the raising of the local corps was left to that redoubtable supporter of the Orange cause, William Blacker, who was then a student at Trinity College, Dublin and still just nineteen years of age. Blacker was granted his commission on 31 October 1796 in a letter from the War Office in Dublin. The Seagoe Yeomanry or 'Blacker's Yeomen' as the unit soon became known, had an initial establishment of one hundred other ranks, three sergeants and one permanent sergeant in the form of Toulerton Lutton of Breagh. Captain Blacker was aided in command by two lieutenants, James Watson and Thomas Mathers, both of whom were Orangemen from the townland of Drumgor. Many of the other members were also Orangemen, some of whom had taken part in the Battle of the Diamond, the previous year.

William Blacker's uncle, George Blacker, Vicar of Seagoe, was also an Orangeman who later rose to the position of County Grand Master. He closely identified himself with the Seagoe Yeomanry and became in effect the unofficial chaplain of the unit. The unit took part in a number of Orange processions adorned in full ceremonial uniform complete with Orange favours and was at one time reviewed by General Lake at Lurgan in 1797. Although many members either belonged to or identified closely with the Orange Order it is incorrect to assume that Roman Catholics were not welcomed within the ranks. Members of the minority community served with distinction alongside their Protestant comrades, but in those days, as now, were subjected to intimidation and threats from the militant sections of the Roman Catholic community. In giving evidence to the House of Commons Select Committee on Orangeism in 1835, William Blacker was asked on the composition of the Seagoe Yeomanry:

Select Committee You command a corps of Yeomanry?
William Blacker I do.
Select Committee Are they exclusively Orangemen?
William Blacker Certainly not.
Select Committee Have you any Roman Catholics in you corps?
William Blacker I knew of one once, I think, I do not know with certainty because I never made any religious distinction.[5]

With the outbreak of the United Irishmen's rebellion in 1798 the Seogoe Yeomanry was ordered to the town of Lisburn to undertake garrison duties and to prevent communication between the rebels of Antrim and Down. Soldiers of 'Blacker's Yeomen' were responsible for capturing Henry Monro, a leading member of the rebels, who was later hanged in Lisburn, with Captain William Blacker and the Seagoe Yeomanry providing the guard. A ballad commemorating the formation and achievements of the Seagoe Yeomanry was written in the 1800s and was reproduced in an early edition of *Seagoe Parish Church Magazine* as follows:

It was in the year '96 these Yeomen did begin
Where they took an oath the boys will keep it free from sin
To back King and Constitution is indeed their whole intent
And Blacker to command them, his mind is fully bent

In Portadown they gathered and marched to Drumcree
Before brave Mr. Manson they soon did all agree
To take the oath of Allegiance, as you may understand
To stand and fight for George our King, while Blacker does command

Out bespoke Captain Blacker like a hero stout and bold
I will clothe you in scarlet most glorious to behold
With a glittering cap and feather your head shall be arrayed
With a good broad sword and musket as you are going to parade

It is for Lieutenant Watson that lives in Portadown
He is a loyal member, few like him can e'er be found
He with his loyal Orangemen united to his King
While other haughty rebels in a halter they will swing

The relative peace enjoyed by Orange areas and the reports that the 'insurrection in the south had been a peasant jacquerie characterised by sectarian killings'[6] made the Orange Order attractive to Protestants of all classes and creeds, including Presby-terians, some of whom had either sympathised with the aims of the United Irishmen or had actually taken part in the fighting. However, once details of the massacres at Vinegar Hill, Wexford Town and the incident at Scullabogue became known the Presbyterians were horrified. In the post-rebellion period this situation assisted greatly in the growth of the Orange Order. In a period of relative peace the Orange Institution's chief role was unconsciously to foster a sense of identity among its members and associates.

Grand Lodge Adopts the Armagh Code

When the Grand Lodge of Ireland next met, on 20 November 1798, the country was still reeling from the affects of the failed United Irishmen's Rebellion. The brethren who met on that occasion could congratulate themselves on the role that the members of the Orange Order had played in defeating the rebellion. Bros. Samuel Montgomery and Harding Gifford reported to the meeting, as charged by the inaugural April meeting, on the codes and regulations as were in operation by County Armagh and County Antrim. Grand Lodge endeavoured to produce a uniform code for all lodges under its jurisdiction. The probable Armagh Code is rendered in Wallace's papers. When compared to the regulations adopted by Portadown District in 1796 the Armagh Code of two years later can be seen to have been heavily influenced by the former. The Portadown code is, arguably a better reasoned, more detailed framework. The rules and regulations of the Orange Order as a whole can be said to have been heavily influenced by the regulations drawn up by the men of Portadown District in August 1796.

III

The Period of Consolidation

Early Demonstrations

IN the years following the 1798 Rebellion the Orangemen of Portadown paraded to the Diamond in celebration of the historic battle that led to the birth of Orangeism. In 1802 there was clear record of a demonstration at the Diamond on 12 July. The brethren assembled at Scotch Street, on the Moy Road, and proceeded in orderly procession to the location of Dan Winter's famous cottage, some four miles distant. After an enjoyable celebration the brethren returned to Portadown via Cosheney and Vinecash.

At a District meeting held on 3 November 1803 it was agreed to provide 'aprons for everybody to walk under, all to bear the following:- King William III on the body of the apron; Number and place of sitting, and all other things as they please, and every Master at our quarterly meeting do appear in their robes of sash and apron or be fined in 13d'.[1] Already codes of dress in Portadown District were becoming more formalised with the introduction of the traditional sashes and aprons. The 'all other things as they please' refers to the various symbols and signs associated with Orangeism.

The religious aspect of the Order was also very much in evidence, with church services being held to mark the occasion of the anniversary of the Battle of the Boyne. Flags were flown from church spires and towers and the bells would often be rung to herald the approach of the anniversary. Often the churches would be decorated with orange and purple flowers. Arches, also made from flowers, would often be strung across streets. In 1804 the Reverend Mr Reed preached to the Portadown brethren at a service at Vinecash Presbyterian Church and the following year a similar service took place at Mullavilly Parish Church. This close link with the church was fostered, among others, by the members of the Blacker family, who were rectors in the Church of Ireland.

The First Service at Drumcree 1807

In 1807 the Reverend Stewart Blacker, the father of William Blacker, preached to the members of Portadown District at a service at Drumcree Parish Church. This was the first recorded Orange service to be held at the church and from henceforth the Orangemen of Portadown attended services regularly at the historic venue. On this first occasion the brethren were headed by men on horseback and on arriving at the flag bedecked Drumcree church were greeted by the rector, the Reverend Stewart Blacker. The Reverend Stewart Blacker was a member of LOL 176, the lodge founded by members of the Verner family in Dublin. At one time the Reverend Stewart Blacker held four different clerical appointments including Vicar of Seagoe and Dean of Leighlin. His brother George Blacker, also a vicar in Seagoe, was also a keen supporter of the Orange cause. According to W. H. Wolsey, George Blacker, together with his nephew, William Blacker, was responsible for penning the fine words and sentiments that are known to brethren as *The Qualifications of an Orangeman*.[2]

'The Most Numerous Procession'

William Blacker wrote of the year 1807 'It was in this year that the most numerous procession of Orange Lodges since 1797 took place'.[3] The location for the county demonstration was in the primatial city of Armagh and as William Blacker went on to describe there was a colourful turnout of Orange brethren and supporters at the occasion:

The entire county was to march past his Grace the Primate at Armagh. More than two-thirds of them met first at Richhill, from whence they proceeded to Armagh, where they were joined at the entrance of the Primate's Demesne by the rest. It was a splendid sight. ...The day was fine, the numerous flags, the scarfs, the diversity of dress – many hundreds being in uniform; the females, full as necessary as the men; the music of every kind made up of nearly as great a variety of instruments as Nebuchadnezzar's Band.[4]

The following year the brethren returned to Vinecash to hear a sermon preached by the Reverend Mr Reed. No records survive of how the celebrations were marked in 1809 but in the year 1810 the District again paraded to Vinecash. The Diamond was the assembly point in 1811 and from there the parade proceeded to Charlemont Fort, where 'James Verner of Church Hill Esq. at the particular request of the body, marched at their head'.[5] Lurgan was the venue for the celebrations in 1812 and in 1813 the venue was Tandragee. In this year lodges not assembling for District Roll Call at 10 o'clock (the time to be taken by Will May's clock) were fined 5s 5d. James Verner's home at Church Hill was the setting for the celebrations of 1814. Thousands of Orangemen from Portadown, Dungannon, Killyman, Loughgall and Armagh gathered at the historic home of the Verner family where the host reviewed the procession which 'marched past him in a regular manner'.[6]

By this time not only were the outward displays of the Orange Order becoming more disciplined and impressive, the internal workings of the Institution were also in the process of being reorganised. Portadown District was represented at County Grand Lodge level by the Worshipful District Master and the District Secretary. These two men were normally accompanied at County meetings by the Masters of three of the private lodges selected on a rota basis in consecutive order.

The Renumbering of Districts
On 6 June 1814 Portadown was again the setting for a decision which had far-reaching consequences for the Orange Institution within the historic County of the Diamond.

At the meeting of the County Grand Lodge, which was held in the Portadown home of Henry Walker it was unanimously agreed to draw lots for the Armagh District warrant numbers. The result was as follows:

District	Warrant No. 1814	1996
Portadown	1	Portadown
Richhill	2	Richhill
Loughgall	3	Loughgall
Tandragee	4	Tandragee
Armagh	5	Armagh
Lurgan	6	Lurgan
Camlough	7	Killylea
Killylea	8	Keady
Newtownhamilton	9	Newtownhamilton
Blackwatertown	10	Markethill
Keady	11	Bessbrook[7]

12 July 1815
Two of County Armagh's most famous Orangemen were absent from the province as the days rolled by in the lead up to the Boyne Anniversaries of 1815. Events elsewhere in Europe, meant that Lt.-Col. William Blacker was in Paris on business, whilst his colleague and brother Orangeman, William Verner of Church Hill, was soon to distinguish himself in one of the most famous battles ever fought – the Battle of Waterloo. Blacker was in the French capital when Napoleon, who had escaped from exile on the island of Elba, was reorganising his forces. Verner, then serving with the 7th Hussars, was seriously wounded on the battlefield of Waterloo on 18 June 1815 and was immediately granted a battlefield commission for his bravery.

The *Belfast News-Letter* carried a full report of the 1815 celebration thus:

Wednesday 12 July 1815, was ushered in in Lurgan, the morning being fine, by the ringers of bells, discharges of small arms, and the display of four Orange flags from the steeple of Shankill Church. After having proceeded to erect a statue of King William, on horseback, and several beautiful arches in the streets, the Orangemen of Lurgan District, proceeded by a handsome musical band, repaired to the seat of Captain

Woolsey, in the vicinity of Portadown, to meet their brethren of the Tandragee and Portadown Districts, who, when united, formed a body of 7000. They then marched to Lurgan, with a display of 120 beautiful flags. The day was spent in conviviality and good-humoured mirth. At about 7 o'clock in the evening they parted, well satisfied with the pleasures of the day, each heart overflowing with gratitude and thankfulness to Divine Providence for its interposition on behalf of these kingdoms by sending the glorious King William as a deliverer to wrest the sceptre from the grasp of a tyrannical bigot.[8]

Further Demonstrations

In the following year the brethren of Portadown proceeded to nearby Tandragee to mark the 12 July anniversary. Brethren were required to assemble at the home of Abraham Dawson at 10 o'clock again under penalty of a fine. On this occasion it was 'the time to be taken from John Sitherwood's clock'.[9] The venue for 1817 is not recorded but a decision was later taken to proceed to 'whatever place our District Master thinks proper'.[10] The record is also blank for 1818 but in 1819 Portadown and Richhill districts combined at Hamiltonsbawn. The 12

July 1820 saw Portadown District parade to Lurgan, two years later Drumcree Parish Church was the venue. In 1823 the celebrations were marked by a procession which 'proceeded to Crow Hill by Scotch Street' and returned via the Diamond and Vinecash.

The year 1823 saw a public addition to the District's activities, which could only have served to enhance the sense of identity which the Orange Order was fostering. Portadown District commenced attendance at services on 5 November, the anniversary of the Gunpowder Plot and the landing of King William III, Prince of Orange, at Brixham. However, over the next few years brethren would find it more and more difficult to openly celebrate their cultural heritage as the government began a clampdown on so-called secret societies. This clampdown manifested itself first in 1824 when it was agreed by the County Grand Lodge that no 12 July demonstrations should take place in County Armagh. This policy was adhered to except in Tandragee where 'a party went out with a drum, but at the request of one of the officers of the Tandragee Yeomanry and a constable, it was taken away'.[11] This was a clear indication of what was to follow.

IV

The Years of Crisis

The Unlawful Associations Act

THE twenty years from 1825 to 1845 was a traumatic time for the Orange Institution. A concerted attempt was made by the authorities to weaken and to destroy the organisation with the introduction of draconian legislation and the setting up of parliamentary inquiries. During this period, the Grand Lodge of Ireland, was dissolved and re-formed and the Order at higher levels in effect became dormant. Once again it was the Orangemen of County Armagh who, remaining unbowed and unbeaten in the face of adversity, took the lead in maintaining Orangeism and the Orange identity.

The first piece of anti-Orange legislation had been introduced in 1823 when the Unlawful Oaths Act was passed. This was followed by the Unlawful Associations Act of 1825. The Bill banned all unlawful associations and had been aimed mainly at Daniel O'Connell's Catholic Association but it also included the Orange Order and the Freemasons. The consequence of the law was that the Grand Lodge of Ireland dissolved itself in March 1825. Some Orange demonstrations were held but they were largely muted affairs and as such the organisation became dormant in some quarters.

In 1825 there was a quiet celebration of the Boyne Anniversary in Portadown with the press reports simply stating that the Orangemen 'walked in procession'.[1] The following year Lurgan was the venue and in 1827 the Portadown brethren walked to the Red Cow Inn to link up with their friends in Lurgan District. By 1828 the Unlawful Associations Act had been allowed to lapse and the Orange Institution was revived in Dublin. However, a new and infinitely more damaging crisis was awaiting only round the corner.

The past few years had seen the revival of the Ribbonmen and their violent activities. Protestants were attacked and their houses, barns and hay burned. These acts led to retaliation and on 12 July 1830 a number of Roman Catholics were burned out of their homes in Maghera. As a result of this renewed violence the government passed the Party Processions Act on 16 August 1832 which in effect made all demonstrations, including Orange ones, illegal.

Colonel Blacker Loses His Commission

On St Patrick's Day in 1833 the Ribbonmen held demonstrations and on St John's Day the Freemasons also held parades. During both of these events the authorities took no action. However, as the month of July approached they were determined to make an example of the Orangemen and they clamped down accordingly. As the forthcoming anniversaries loomed ever closer, Grand Lodge exhorted its members not to break the law and Colonel Blacker himself advised local Orangemen to refrain from the public celebration of the Battle of the Boyne. The rank and file, though, were in no mood for compromise, believing it essential that they should mark the auspicious occasion. On 12 July 1833 the Orangemen assembled in Portadown from where they paraded the two miles to Carrickblacker. As the Orangemen gathered on the front lawn at Carrickblacker House they were addressed by Lt.-Col. Blacker. The *Evening Packet* gave an in depth report of the event as follows:

> Lurgan and Portadown were decorated and in both places the bells continued ringing for several hours. In the course of the day vast numbers of the Protestants from each of the above towns and the surrounding country, many of them on horseback, proceeded with music etc., to pay their respects

to that highly esteemed gentleman, Colonel Blacker, of Carrick. The colonel, who, together with his lady, received them with very great courtesy, addressed the multitude in terms of the kindest and most friendly admonition on the danger of exposing themselves to their enemies and requested them to return to their homes peaceably without giving or taking offence, and without delay. This was acceded to with loud and grateful cheers and the assembly, which could not have amounted to less than 20,000 of all ages and sexes, went off in different directions, the utmost quietness prevailing. The private celebrations of the day were most numerous.[2]

The colonel's wife, Mrs Anne Blacker, showed her support for the demonstration by wearing an orange coloured dress, whilst some of the maids of the house were adorned with orange lilies in their hair. Stewart Blacker, the colonel's nephew, was also in attendance. The Orangemen had gathered for about fifteen minutes on the front lawn of Carrick House before peacefully dispersing, but as far as the authorities were concerned this was deemed an unpardonable offence. Fourteen of those who took part in the monster gathering were arrested and committed to stand trial at the Armagh Assizes. Three were bound over to keep the peace by the court, whilst the remainder were freed.

The news of the trial was greeted with disdain in the local community and effigies of John Hancock JP, the man responsible for gathering the evidence against the Orangemen, were burned in Tandragee and Portadown. The authorities at Dublin Castle instituted an inquiry into the whole affair which had taken place at Carrickblacker and in other areas where Orangemen had paraded in defiance of the law. The results of these inquiries were of course heavily weighted against the cause of Orangeism. William Blacker was dismissed as a Justice of the Peace for County Armagh, on the advice of Lord Gosford, for allowing the Orangemen to demonstrate at Carrickblacker, even though he had advised them to disperse. His close friend and fellow prominent Orangeman, William Verner, a veteran of

Waterloo, resigned his commission in disgust at the decision of the inquiry.

On 5 November 1833 a few months after the 'illegal' gathering at Carrickblacker the brethren of Portadown, undeterred by threats of fines or imprisonment, assembled at 'the head of the walk' and proceeded to Drumcree Church to commemorate the Gunpowder Plot. This church parade took place 'without flags or music' but 'in full uniform'.[3] By this time the term uniform had come to mean Orange sashes.

Portadown Orangemen Arrested
In July of the following year the situation was no different with many Orangemen being arrested for daring to celebrate the civil and religious liberty that King William III had gained by his victory at the Boyne. The brethren had decided to meet at Ballybay Bridge at 11 o'clock from where they paraded to Scotch Street via the townland of Cohara. On the return route the Orangemen walked by way of Annakera and Druminally to their dispersal point at Selshion Turns. The police made notes on those who took part and a number of names were forwarded by Charles Atkinson, Chief Constable in a 'return of those identified by the police that marched in the procession in Portadown on 12 July 1834'. The following names were listed: 'John Hamilton DM, second offence; Thomas Dawson, second offence; Robert M. Winters, second offence; George Mathers, second offence; Samuel Faloon, second offence; Mortimer Woodhouse, ? Lewis, ? Watson and William Lyons'.[4]

The first name on the list, John Hamilton, was the Worshipful District Master of Portadown District who had held the office from 1830 to 1835 and the second name, Thomas Dawson, was the Portadown District Secretary from 1830 to 1839. At the March meeting of the District Lodge 'It was ordered that all expenses over two pounds for the purpose of defending our brethren at the ensuing Assizes is to be defrayed by the several lodges of the District.'[5]

In the run up to the celebrations of 1835, the Grand Lodge of Ireland ordered Orangemen throughout the country not to parade on 12 July, but rather to mark the historic occasion quietly. In Portadown this request was further supported by a resolution passed by the County Armagh Grand Lodge. The Portadown Orangemen were, however, determined to mark the anniversary of the Battle of the Boyne with a parade.

The Celebrations of 1835

On 12 July the Portadown Orangemen duly congregated in the town from where they marched to Drumcree Parish Church. At the church they listened to an eloquent sermon expertly delivered by the Reverend Charles Alexander. According to the *Newry Telegraph* the procession was 'not distinguished by either music or flags nor did it exhibit any insignia of the Order, except a few who wore Orange scarfs'.[6] An Orange arch had been erected across Woodhouse Street which was later removed by the police on the orders of Mr Curran Woodhouse, a local magistrate. After the service at Drumcree, the Orangemen 'dispersed peacefully, with, not the slightest disturbance having occurred, or any breach of the peace committed'.[7]

The following day Portadown Orangemen were again determined to parade but the authorities, alarmed at the prospect of so many Orangemen flouting the law with virtual impunity, moved quickly to redress the situation. They ordered the 2nd Dragoons and a company of the 33rd Foot Regiment from Newry to garrison the town to prevent an outward display by the Orange society. In the meantime, a number of the town's dignitaries had intervened and persuaded the Orangemen to disperse. Later the same day it became known that a large contingent of Orangemen had gathered in Lurgan with the purpose of marching to Portadown to meet their Portadown brethren. The *Newry Telegraph* reported that:

2,000 Orangemen were on the march from Lurgan, in full procession, upon which the magistrates posted the whole force under their command at the bridge (at Edenderry) horse, foot and police and a terrible collision was expected. However Col. Blacker, whose excellent conduct as a peacemaker throughout the day deserves great praise, came forward and undertook to stop the body of men

from Lurgan, provided the troops were removed. His undertaking was accepted and he was successful on prevailing them to return home.[8]

The 1835 Select Committee on Orangeism

The events in Portadown and elsewhere and the allegations of an Orange conspiracy in England linked with the Duke of Cumberland, led to the setting up of a parliamentary commission, charged with investigating the Orange Order. Leading members of the Institution, including William Blacker, (whose deposition was one of the longest amounting to some forty pages) and his nephew Stewart Blacker gave evidence to the committee. The report listed the number of working lodges within the whole of Ireland, where they sat and what district they came under. Also listed were all Grand officers, County officers and Worshipful Masters of private lodges. Portadown District's Worshipful Master was listed as J. Hamilton who lived in the town and the lodges within the District were as follows: 7, 8, 9, 10, 13, 18, 19, 20, 25, 31, 35, 40, 56, 58, 78, 80, 81, 89, 99, 107, 172, 417, 516, 948 and 1301.

The main consequence of the commission was that the Duke of Cumberland was forced to dissolve military lodges in England and on 14 April 1836 the Grand Lodge of Ireland followed suit.

It was left to the County that was the home of Orangeism to take the lead and on 13 June a special meeting was called at which many prominent Portadown Orange brethren were in attendance. To the Portadown brethren the Orange Order meant everything; it was a bulwark of the Protestant religion and through their membership they supported peace and the good order of the realm. They were determined to keep the Order in existence and rejected outright any possible dropping of the title Orange (a possible outcome briefly hinted at in some quarters). Accordingly a resolution was passed which stated:

That the Grand Lodge of Ireland, having dissolved itself, of the business of the Institution in this county, be entrusted as in its early days, to the Grand Lodge of the same until the Grand Lodge resumes its function; that Colonel Verner having declined being Grand Master of this county, we do hereby elect Lieut-Colonel Blacker to that office.[9]

William Blacker held this position until the following year when Lord Roden was elected, in his absence, by a remnant of Grand Lodge meeting at Dawson Street in Dublin.

In 1836 a small number of Portadown Orangemen openly celebrated the 12 July anniversary in contravention of a resolution that had been adopted at a meeting of the District on 25 June 1836. A committee was later set up to investigate the conduct of these brethren whose actions were subsequently condemned in the report. From 1838 to 1844 there are no minutes of Portadown District as in effect the Order had gone into virtual abeyance because of the dissolution of Grand Lodge. There were a few small gatherings of Orangemen but these were largely muted affairs with no regalia, music or any open display of the symbols of the Order.

On 31 May 1845 the Party Processions Act expired, much to the satisfaction of Orangemen who prepared to celebrate the anniversary of the victory gained by their forefathers at the Boyne.

V

The Right to March

THE County Armagh demonstration of 1845 as held in Portadown – the event led Lord Gosford, in a letter to Dublin Castle, to comment thus:

> I have this moment seen Mr Singleton RM, who informs me that on Saturday last 80 Orange Lodges, 60 stand of colours, each with Fife and Drums, 1800 Orangemen wearing scarfs and accompanied by ten thousand persons marched in procession through the town of Portadown on the 12th.[1]

The following year the venue was Tandragee, where a newspaper reporter counted '150 flags'. In the same year it was agreed at the District Lodge that on 5 November each private lodge should 'go to the nighest Church and not to have either flags or music with them'.[2] These 'Gunpowder Plot' services survived until recently when they were changed to the Reformation Sunday church services. On 12 July 1847 Lurgan and Portadown Districts met just outside Portadown for their celebrations. In attendance was Lt.-Col. William Blacker, the famous Orange leader.

On 9 July 1848 Portadown Orangemen attended a church service at St Mark's Church. Records show that a total of 769 persons were present, and the collection amounted to 7s. 2d. The 12 July demonstration of 1848 was a particularly enthusiastic one as this report in the *Armagh Guardian* 17 July clearly shows:

> Portadown – In this loyal town the ever memorable anniversary of the glorious 12th July, was ushered in by the ringing of the church bells, the firing of guns etc. From an early hour in the morning, the fife and drum could be heard in all directions warning the brethren to assemble at their respective lodge rooms; and at ten o'clock the several

lodges headed by their masters, with banners and music, began to pour into the town.

Again the venue was midway between Lurgan and Portadown, this time at the little hamlet of Bluestone, where the brethren assembled in a field kindly loaned for the occasion by Mr Robinson. Several Roman Catholics from the area, attended the celebrations without any hint of animosity whatsoever, indeed they were welcomed openly. The report on the celebrations in the *Armagh Guardian* continued:

> It is impossible to convey an adequate idea of the scene that now presented itself, 58 lodges, numbering at least 1,250 men who composed the procession, besides there could not have been less than 15,000 followers. The banners, which were mostly new, together with a large and handsome orange flag on the church tower; the numerous fifes and drums, and the dense mass of people, altogether rendered the scene a most imposing one.

During this time the District Lodge was well and truly active, passing a number of resolutions and bye-laws with which the individual private lodges had to comply. On 13 June 1849 a resolution was passed forbidding publicans from holding the office of Worshipful Master. It read as follows: 'That such Masters of Lodges in this District as are publicans do now resign the office of Master of said lodge, a successor to be elected at the next meeting of such lodge. It is also resolved that no lodge do from henceforth meet for the business of Orangemen in any Public House'.[3]

At the District Lodge meeting held on 31 May 1850 a motion, clearly influenced by the Party Processions Act, was passed:

That we have heard certain unfounded reports of Lodge 948 in our District, setting forth the intention of the members of the same to burn their flags, sashes etc. Now we the several Masters assembled in the District Lodge declare all such rumours to be false; and further declare our unanimous determination to stand by the Orange Institution as heretofore, notwithstanding the recent Act of Parliament passed against us.[4]

Celebrations continued throughout the 1850s with nothing remarkable of note distinguishing the demonstrations. Due to the stance taken against the Party Processions Act during this period of uncertainty, Portadown became known as the 'Orange Citadel'.

On 12 July 1854 a religious service was held at Tartaraghan. In 1857 Portadown District assembled on 13 July 'bringing their music but no colours or banners or any other emblems that might give offence or make a breach of the law'.[5] Once more the authorities were beginning to act against the Orange Order and as in the 1830s introduced legislation banning Orange Parades. In the aftermath of the Battle of Dolly's Brae on 12 July 1849 a Party Processions Act had been passed in 1850 and this was to be followed by even more stringent legislation a decade later.

The Party Emblems Act
The decade of the 1860s was a traumatic time for the Orange Order in Portadown, beginning as it did with the passing of The Party Emblems Act of 1860 and ending with the tragic death of an innocent young Portadown loyalist in Bridge Street, Edenderry on 1 July 1869. The Party Emblems Act, introduced in the aftermath of a serious riot at Derrymacash, near Lurgan, banned all displays of flags, emblems or symbols as well as the playing of music in public street, place or road. In addition any public parade, meeting or demonstration was deemed to be illegal and anyone taking part was liable to arrest. Together with the Party Processions Act of 1850, these two pieces of legislation made it virtually impossible for Orangemen to legally commemorate the anniversary of the Battle of the Boyne by any public dis-

play or even by the innocuous ritual of lighting traditional July bonfires. The passing of the 1860 Act at first had little effect on the Orangemen of Portadown, but as the decade progressed the law was enforced more and more rigorously.

A report from the *Newry Telegraph* describes the celebrations of 12 July 1861:

From an early hour in the morning numbers of gaily dressed people continued to congregate in the town, but the utmost order prevailed. Several parties with fifes and drums passed through the town en route to the various lodges and through the unexceptional arrangements made and carried out by Joseph Cox, RM, the police have remained under cover in the Loan Fund Co's (Ltd). premises all day.

The 12 July 1862 was marked by the visit of Orangemen from Belfast. The *Newry Telegraph* reported that 'At least 1,000 of the fellowship, comprising several lodges assembled a little way out of the town. We understand the police took the names of several of the processionists'.[6] It was a portent of things to come. The following year there was a gathering of Orangemen in Portadown but in nearby Gilford eight millworkers were arrested for 'parading behind fifes and drums when leaving work on 14 July'.[7]

The demonstration of 1864 was again an enthusiastic one 'The town was filled with large numbers of well dressed young men and women. The thoroughfares were literally crammed. The local Head-Constable Wilson and a party of constabulary were on duty but not a single case for calling for their services occurred.'[8] The following year the celebrations were of a similar character but those in 1866 were marred by the arrest, under the Party Processions Act, of four Orangemen from the area. They were sent for trial at the local assizes with the Bill of Indictment as reported in the *Portadown News* 28 July, as follows:

The Queen Verses Thomas Hoy, of Artabracka, Mercer Steenson, of Ballinary, Robert Ruddock, of Richmount, and Henry Mercer, of The Diamond, for committing a breach of the Party Processions Act, by meeting and parading on the public road, wearing party colours, and playing music, which was calculated to provoke animosity between different classes of Her Majesty's subjects.

Nothing of course could have been further from the truth. The Orangemen were not out to provoke anyone, but rather to enjoy and celebrate their distinctive culture and heritage. Roman Catholics had often attended these Orange parades and had not been offended by them. It was once again a heavy handed approach to a problem that did not really exist. The arresting police officer – Constable Birney – then gave evidence to the court on the arrest of the Orangemen:

I remember the 12th July. I saw Mercer Steenson that day on horseback. He had orange ribbons on his horse's ears. He was not wearing any party emblems himself. I saw Henry Mercer with an orange sash on him that day, and he was also playing on a fife. I am not exactly sure of Robert Ruddock. I cannot positive swear to him. I saw Thomas Hoy riding on a horse, and he had his ears decked out with something bordering on an orange colour. He was in a crowd where persons were wearing party colours which were calculated to provoke animosity.

The absurdity of the trial is self evident, two men arrested for probably one of the most trivial offences in the history of the British legal system – for having placed orange rosettes in their horses' ears and another man arrested for playing a musical instrument in public!

In 1867 thousands again thronged the streets to celebrate the Boyne anniversary. Despite the draconian legislation as evidenced above, the people would not be deterred from marking this great occasion. The *Portadown News* 6 July, reported:

The Twelfth of 1867 has passed, and (in this town at least) has been characterised by orderly conduct. It was ushered in by the ringing of the church bell, and the sound of fife and drum, the ringing and beating of which

were continued at intervals throughout the entire day. We are happy to say that, notwithstanding the great numbers that thronged our streets, there was nothing unpleasant to mar this honoured anniversary.

Waringstown was the venue for 12 July celebrations of 1868, where William Johnston of Ballykilbeg, the leader of the campaign against the Act, addressed the assemblage. Johnston had been arrested for leading an Orange procession to Bangor. According to the *Portadown News* of 18 July it was 'the largest ever seen in that neighbourhood'. Most of the Portadown brethren and supporters travelled by train but a few availed themselves of a new carriage service laid on by Mrs Margaret Grew who owned the Queen's Arms Hotel. Forty policemen from County Meath were present but the gathering passed off peacefully. However, the following year, a tragedy occurred when a young man from Portadown was shot dead by police in Edenderry on 1 July during the traditional burning of the effigy of Lundy.

The Fatal Affray of 1 July 1869

The young man was Thomas Watson aged just sixteen years of age who was at the time an employee at the nearby Ulster Railway Station. The events which surrounded young Watson's death, had serious repercussions in the town, where the incident later became known as the 'Fatal Affray'. Questions were asked in the House of Commons, letters appeared in the national newspapers and the inspector who had given the order to open fire, was later charged with causing the boy's death.

The events of that fateful day began with the actions of a few children who had been innocently building a bonfire at the Quarry Turns, at the junction of the Killycomain and Gilford Roads. On 1 July, in time honoured fashion, they set fire to the small pile of wood, only to see the flames stamped out by an unarmed police patrol comprising four constables. The senior constable stated that lighting a bonfire was illegal and called on the children to disperse immediately. A large crowd of parents soon gathered at the bonfire to remonstrate with the police. Again the senior constable insisted that the crowd disperse and began to threaten the onlookers with gaol sentences if they did not. The crowd immediately began to throw stones and attacked the police who quickly withdrew to the direction of Edenderry Square and to the safety of the RIC Barracks in Woodhouse Street.

The *Belfast News Letter*, dated 3 July, reported: 'They at once repaired to the barracks, from which they reissued with the whole of the available force – some eight or nine men under the command of Sub-Inspector Nunan. Even the mounted constable attached to the station was brought out, armed with his revolver.' A very ugly scene was now developing in Edenderry with hundreds of Orangemen, who had been at a Lambeg drumming match, coming into the Square. As news of the provocative and heavy-handed police action spread a riot situation ensued with the police falling back under a hail of stones. Inspector Nunan then gave the order for the police to open fire on the protesters. The first volley was fired in the air, but had little effect in dispersing the crowd. At the second volley, Thomas Watson, who had been standing in a shop doorway near Hamilton Robb's, was fatally wounded as a bullet tore through his left breast. The unfortunate Watson had just finished his evening shift as a porter at the Railway Station and had inadvertently been caught up in the disturbances. Nearby, William Girvan, a nineteen year old Roman Catholic, from Coalisland, was seriously injured.

Order was finally restored in the early hours but as the *Newry Commercial Telegraph* of 3 July reported: 'The consternation amongst the inhabitants is immense. The police dare not leave the barracks; but at twelve o'clock quietness began to prevail.'

The funeral of Thomas Watson was a huge affair with almost the entire population of the town either watching the cortege or taking part in the procession as it made its way to Seagoe Cemetery. There was a large Orange presence at the funeral which received full coverage in the *Belfast News Letter* of 5 July: 'The brethren closest to the hearse wore white sashes and white hat bands trimmed with black, and those bringing up the next part of the solemn and imposing procession wore black sashes and hat bands trimmed with white. Then came a large body of the society wearing the full insignia of their Order. The members of the following Orange Lodges attended:- LOL Numbers 7, 8, 9, 10, 13, 18, 19, 20, 25, 31, 35, 40, 56, 58, 78, 80, 81, 89, 99, 107, 417, 516, 948, and 1301... After leaving the burying-ground, the Orangemen marched in procession into the town, and on reaching the front of the Protestant Church (St Mark's) they halted, and then quietly dispersed.'

Sub-Inspector Nunan was subsequently tried for the manslaughter of Thomas Watson with the court finally being held at the Dundalk Assizes. This court was chosen as being the most likely to find a favourable verdict for the inspector. Nunan was not surprisingly found 'Not Guilty' much to the consternation of the local press especially the *Portadown News* 16 July 1870 which commented on the verdict thus: 'Sub-Inspector Nunan has been – well – *tried* at the Dundalk Assizes, and a jury of his *fellows* have brought him in "Not Guilty" of the manslaughter of poor Watson. We believe however that any impartial man that reads the evidence ... must say that the verdict was such as might expect from a Dundalk jury'. On the affair as a whole, the newspaper concluded that: 'the police certainly acted in the matter with great indiscretion and imprudence.'

A year after this unfortunate incident and thanks largely to the stand made by William Johnston of Ballykilbeg and his 'Right To March' campaign, the Party Processions Act was repealed and Orangemen were once again able to openly celebrate the anniversary of the Battle of the Boyne without fear of arrest.

Orangemen at Carrickblacker

With freedom once more restored to Orange parades the brethren of Portadown District attended a mammoth gathering of the Order, on 12 July 1870, at Carrickblacker House. Even before the parade got under way, the town was already resonating to the sound of fife and drum. At midnight the local churches in the town – Seagoe, St Mark's and Drumcree – had marked the beginning of the 'Twelfth' celebrations by the constant pealing of their church bells. Many bonfires had been started, but in the absence of legislation, there was to be no hint of the unease which marred the celebrations of the previous year. Indeed there was a carnival atmosphere in the air, as the report in the *Portadown and Lurgan News* made clear:

> The 12th of July ... was celebrated in this town and neighbourhood with an earnestness and enthusiasm never equalled on any previous occasion. In the recollection of the oldest inhabitant no demonstration ever held in Portadown surpassed this one in numbers, enthusiasm or respectability. From a most untimely hour the town was alive with sympathisers to the cause who seemed determined to take as much fun out of the day as possible.

Altogether around two hundred lodges took part in the demonstration including many from areas in Tyrone and County Down. The following Orange Districts were represented at Carrickblacker: Armagh, Portadown, Lurgan, Tandragee, Newtownhamilton, Keady, Killylea, Loughgall, Richhill and Scarva. Supporters travelled from all over the county and beyond, all taking advantage of the cheap day excursion by train.

The railway station in Edenderry was the meeting point for the Orangemen who then proceeded along the two mile route to the demonstration field at Carrickblacker. All along the route there were thousands of supporters cheering the marchers on their way. The *Portadown and Lurgan News* estimated the crowds in Portadown to be in the region of 50,000 and those at Carrickblacker House around 30,000. Even though it was obvious that the proceedings would pass off peacefully, the authorities stationed a company of the 47th Regiment under the command of Captains Newman and Dent, at the Brownlow Arms Hotel in Lurgan, in case of any trouble. Their services were not required.

The following year Portadown District paraded to Castledillon, where Major Stewart Blacker led the proceedings. The speakers at this demonstration included the Reverend Charles King Irwin – a former

District Master of Portadown – James Jones, J. H. Fullerton and C. Waring. In 1872 the entire County gathered at Ballylough near Lurgan where the main speaker was Edward Wingfield Verner MP. Again these demonstrations passed off peacefully as was usually the case as far as Orange demonstrations were concerned.

The Visit of the Canadian Orangemen
The 12 July celebrations of 1873 were perhaps some of the most distinctive in the history of Portadown District for two very different reasons. In early July a delegation of Canadian brethren who had been visiting various parts of Ireland received a warm welcome in Portadown. The two men were D'Arcy Boulton, DGM of British America and his colleague Herbert S. McDonald, Provincial Grand Master of Ontario East. The men were accompanied by Stewart Blacker and attended a reception in their honour at the Town Hall. In his welcoming address Stewart Blacker made reference to the formation of the Orange Institution in the nearby village of the Diamond and to the growth of the Order in Portadown. The major then pointed out that he wished to perform a very special ceremony on his Canadian brethren whereupon he opened a bag and took out an Orange sash that had been worn by the first Grand Master of the Order in County Armagh, his late uncle, Lt.-Col. William Blacker. He then invested the Canadians with the historic sash to the uproarious applause from the floor. The delegates remained at Carrickblacker overnight before they continued on their tour with a visit to Armagh.

Armagh was the venue for the County demonstration and the Portadown brethren assembled at the Fair Green from whence they paraded to the railway station in Edenderry. The *Portadown News* dated 26 July relates how 'the District was well represented, there being 18 stand of colours, and the members of each lodge were dressed in the full insignia of the Order'. The speeches in the field at Ballinahone were delivered by Bro. Stewart Blacker, Bro. Richard Lilburn, the editor of the *Belfast News Letter* and by one of the visiting Canadian delegates, Bro. Dr Oronhyoteka, a

Mohawk Indian chief. The proceedings had been peaceful in all accounts but others elsewhere in Portadown had been using the time to prepare an ambush on the Portadown Orangemen as they returned home.

Trouble at the Tunnel

The Portadown Orangemen returned from Armagh at half past six in the evening and they marched through the town before they dispersed. The route of three lodges, comprising a total of 86 Orangemen, happened to take them through the 'Tunnel' area and in that direction they proceeded with flags unfurled and with drums and fifes playing. The *Portadown News*, 26 July, described the incident thus:

> They got the length of River Lane without the least molestation and it was beginning to be hoped that the inhabitants of this unenviably-notorious locality would manifest for once a forbearance peculiarly foreign to their training and inculcations... At this place most wanton and unprovoked, but eminently characteristic assault – characteristic insomuch as it was of the most dastardly and despicably sneakish description – was made upon them [Orangemen] from the backs and windows of the houses with stones, brick-bats, large pieces of broken crockery and every conceivable description of missile, all of which were thrown with a violence and continuity perfectly compatible with the skulking poltroonery that dictated such a plan for waylaying a number of peaceable men whose only crime was that they were Protestants and loyal subjects.

A number of the Orangemen as well as police officers were wounded in the unprovoked and obviously well planned attack. Recovering from their surprise the Orangemen defended themselves vigorously and eventually they re-formed to continue their parade through the 'Tunnel' to their homes. This was possibly the first recorded account of Orangemen being attacked in this area.

Carleton Street Orange Hall

During the early 1870s meetings of Portadown District were being held in the Techni-

cal School. However, with an outlook obviously on the future, and to further strengthen and maintain an Orange presence in the town, Portadown Orangemen began to make provision for an Orange hall, where Orange brethren from all over Portadown and further afield, could hold meetings under more convivial surroundings. The foundation stone was laid in 1873 and the hall was opened two years later in 1875. A detailed history of Carleton Street Orange Hall follows in Chapter XIV.

The Life of Major Stewart Blacker

With the death in 1855 of Lt.-Col. William Blacker, the celebrated 'Bard of Armagh' the Orange Institution was dealt a severe blow. However, his nephew, Stewart Blacker, himself an Orange stalwart from an early age, carried on the family tradition of unstinting loyalty and service to the cause of Orangeism.

During the troubled times of the 1830s Stewart Blacker gave his wholehearted support to Portadown District and was present at the gathering of Orangemen at Carrickblacker in 1833. He also attended a Portadown District Lodge meeting held on 28 December 1835. The same year Major Blacker was one of those who was called to give evidence to the parliamentary commission charged with investigating the Institution. Stewart Blacker went on to become the Grand Secretary of the Grand Orange Lodge of Ireland, a position he was to hold for many years. He was always willing to help his Orange brethren, often allowing demonstrations to be held at Carrickblacker. He was also, along with his sister, Hester Anne Von Stieglitz, one of the chief contributors to the financing of the new Orange hall in Portadown in 1875.

Stewart Blacker suffered from ill health throughout his later life and died on 16 December 1881 aged 68 years. The news of his demise was received with great sorrow throughout the area especially amongst the brethren of his own private lodge, Carrickblacker LOL 41. At a meeting of The Grand Orange Lodge of Ireland, held in York Street, Belfast, a message of sympathy was passed which was forwarded to Stewart's sister. Grand Lodge also put on record the 'deep sense all entertained of the life-long services rendered to the cause of Protestantism by their departed and valued brother whose name and memory would ever be cherished in the annals of the Orange Order'.[9]

The funeral of Stewart Blacker took place on 22 December 1881 and according to the *Portadown and Lurgan News* of the following Saturday 'The Orange Institution, of which he was an honoured and beloved member were present in considerable strength and the entire vast assemblage, extending as it did over a mile along the road, testified that his labours on behalf of Protestantism were not forgotten'. Included amongst them were Edward Wingfield Verner, the County Grand Master of Armagh and William Johnston of Ballykilbeg. The following lodges from Portadown District took part in the funeral cortege as it made its way from Carrickblacker to the family burying ground at Seagoe: LOL 7, 8, 9, 10, 13, 18, 19, 20, 25, 31, 35, 40, 56, 58, 78, 80, 81, 89, 99, 107, 172, 417, 516, 948, 1238, and 1301.

Two years after his death, the memory of Major Blacker was kept alive by the formation of two Orange lodges in Portadown District. One bearing the title Stewart Blacker's Crimson Banner LOL 927 was formed on 7 August 1883 under a dispensation from Edward Wingfield Verner. The lodge was always a small one and ceased to function a few years later in 1906, (LOL 927 now functions in Bessbrook District). The second lodge took out warrant number LOL 1654 and was known as Blacker's True Blues. This lodge functioned until 1890 when it exchanged its warrant for LOL 89.

The death of Major Stewart Blacker was reported in the *Portadown and Lurgan News* of 17 December 1881:

The columns of this paper have never announced a death more universally regretted than that of the late owner of the Carrickblacker Estate near this town. On Friday morning, about four o'clock, Major Stewart Blacker breathed his last in the fine old house in which he had spent his lifetime... At his last most memorable appearance in public the Portadown audience showed their appreciation by every man rising to his feet and as he passed cheering him to the echo. 'Blacker of Carrickblacker' mentioned at any of the numerous political meetings of the North in days gone by was enough to stir up a ring of enthusiastic applause. It was everywhere the same. By his death; the Conservative cause loses a trusty and tried friend and as a high officer in the Orange Institution he nobly stood by that body... The announcement of his death was received with feelings of profound regret in Portadown, where he was highly and deservedly respected.

VI

The Home Rule Crisis

The Building of Orange Halls

THE growth of Irish nationalism in the later decades of the nineteenth century gave a new significance to the Orange Order's place in the Protestant community. Protestants, again fearful of developments threatening their peace and prosperity, looked afresh at the Orange Order as the symbol of their community and the vehicle for its defence. As a result the Orange Order grew in membership and in strength and became more visible as the symbol of an identity, through the trend of constructing Orange halls. Private lodges, which hitherto had held meetings in the homes of members, acquired most of the halls in the District between 1873 and 1914 . A period that saw the attempted introduction of no fewer than three Home Rule Bills to Ireland.

The first purpose built Orange hall in County Armagh was that at Derrinraw which was opened on 16 January 1873 by members of LOL 10. This was followed by the opening of Carleton Street Orange Hall in 1875. The opening dates for Orange halls in the Portadown area during this period are as follows:

LOL 10	1873	LOL 172	1884
LOL 7	1891	LOL 107	1895
LOL 26	1897	LOL 81	1899
LOL 9	1904	LOL 35	1905
LOL 22	1908	LOL 371	1910
LOL 339	1911	LOL 8	1912
LOL 31	1912	LOL 20	1913
LOL 18	1914		

Over the next three decades the Orange Order was at the forefront in opposing the implementation of Home Rule and nowhere was this opposition as strong as that in Portadown. The town continued to maintain its sobriquet of the 'Orange Citadel'. Membership of the various lodges in Portadown District saw an unprecedented rise during the last two decades of the nineteenth century and many new Orange lodges were formed in these years of uncertainty. The 12 July celebrations carried on as usual and these became the focus for the growing opposition to the Liberals' policy of granting Home Rule to Ireland.

The 12 July celebrations of 1880 were held in Portadown whilst those of the following year were held in the small village of Killylea. Lurgan was the venue for the Armagh County demonstration of 1882 and in 1883 the brethren returned to the tree-lined demesne at Carrickblacker. This year also saw Portadown District appoint Bro. W. J. Freeburn as District bugler to carry out ceremonial duties and it was also in 1883 that the issue of a District banner was first raised. Discipline was the strict order of the day with the District minutes recording a number of fines on lodges and individuals for various misdemeanours as follows:

Lodges not answering roll-call in field	£1
Lodges not answering roll-call in Carleton St. on return	£2
Lodges playing drums in field during meeting	10 shillings
Lodges breaking off in procession	£2
Lodges not attending demonstration	£2

These fines were heavily enforced even to the point of asking lodges to hand in their warrants if they did not comply. One man was suspended for a period of 99 years for a serious breach of discipline and another was suspended for a period of nine years.[1]

During this period the nationalist tactic which became known as 'boycott' after Captain Charles Boycott, the agent for Lord Erne's Mayo estate, was initiated. The captain was shunned by the local people and it was only with the intervention of Orangemen that the potato and corn crop in the area was harvested. Some of these Orangemen were from Portadown and one in particular Bro. George Locke, was highly praised for his efforts by officers of the Grand Lodge of Ireland.

In addition to the normal 12 July celebrations there were also a number of election rallies and other demonstrations in which members of Portadown District took part in. One of these was to have tragic consequences for one young Portadown Orangeman from Meadow Lane who now lies buried in Seagoe Cemetery.

The Death of Samuel James Giffin
1 January 1884

Giffin was just eighteen years old when he was fatally wounded at a demonstration at Dromore, County Tyrone, on New Year's Day 1884. He lived in Meadow Lane and was employed as a flax dresser in the local weaving industry. Like his fellow citizens, Samuel was naturally concerned about the possibility of a Home Rule parliament in Dublin, in which the Protestant religion, culture and heritage would be overwhelmed in a largely Roman Catholic dominated state. Meetings and demonstrations were held all over Ulster in which the Orange Order, as usual, played a leading role. One such meeting, typical of many, was held in the Tyrone village of Dromore on 1 January 1884.

A large contingent of Orangemen, including the young Giffin, travelled the fifty odd miles from Portadown by train, to join the mammoth gathering at Dromore. In order to create as much trouble as possible the local Home Rulers also organised a counter-demonstration and openly taunted the gathering Orangemen. A thin line of RIC officers, aided by Hussars, kept the two sides apart for most of the day. Unfortunately, whilst the Orangemen were dispersing and as they were making their way to the train station, they come under violent abuse from the nationalists. In the words of the *Portadown & Lurgan News* dated 5 January, the nationalists goaded the loyalists '...with their disloyal and party cries.' Soon they began to throw stones, bricks and other missiles at the peacefully dispersing Orangemen. After

being on the receiving end of a vicious and unprovoked attack, some of the younger elements, including Samuel Giffin, charged at the nationalists. The police closed ranks and also fixed bayonets to prevent them from reaching the nationalists. As Giffin made to break through the lines, he was fatally injured by a policeman's bayonet. Giffin was brought to a local house for treatment, where he remained until his death, eight days later, on 9 January 1884.

An inquest was held into the tragic death, with the jury finding that Giffin had died as a result of a bayonet wound. Although it had been a policeman who had fatally injured Giffin, the jury were unable to ascertain exactly who had administered the fatal bayonet wound. The papers of the day, put the blame for the tragic incident fairly and squarely on the shoulders of the government, for allowing the counter-demonstration to take place, when it was already known that an Orange meeting was being held in the same village.

In the funeral procession later in the week, which the *Portadown & Lurgan News* described as '...one of the most imposing ceremonies witnessed in Portadown for many years...' the body of Samuel Giffin was borne through his home town. As the cortege wound its way from the deceased's home in Meadow Lane via High Street, Bridge Street and Edenderry to the cemetery at Seagoe, thousands lined the route, whilst hundreds followed behind the coffin. Many Orangemen from Portadown District and surrounding areas walked in silent tribute to their fallen brother. The funeral service was held in Seagoe Parish Church and was conducted by the Rector of Portadown Parish, the Reverend Dr Augustine Fitzgerald. After the service the body of the late Samuel Giffin was finally laid to rest. Later a memorial tablet was erected on the youth's grave which, long after the incident has been forgotten, serves as a lasting reminder of that fateful New Year's Day in 1884.

Ulster Will Fight

The 12 July demonstration of 1884 was held in the County Down town of Newry where there was a huge turnout of Armagh and

Down Orange lodges. The emphasis of the proceedings was, naturally enough, directed against Gladstone and the Liberal Party for their policy on Home Rule. The following year the Armagh brethren again converged on Carrickblacker House, the former residence of the recently deceased Major Stewart Blacker, where there was more condemnation of Home Rule.

This growing opposition to the Home Rule Bill was characterised by Lord Randolph Churchill with his words 'Ulster will fight and Ulster will be right'. In a tour of the Province he stated that if Home Rule was implemented 'the Orange card would be the one to play'. This, however, turned out not to be necessary as in June 1886 the Bill was defeated in the House of Commons, much to the joy of Orangemen throughout the Province. However, its spectre still hung over the loyal men and women who had opposed it so vehemently. In the same month the Grand Orange Lodge of Ireland directed its County lodges to order private lodges to provide whatever drill instruction the law permitted. Home Rule was still denounced on every available occasion, especially when that great favourite of Portadown Orangemen, Colonel Edward James Saunderson was in attendance. During those years the 12 July also became a focal point for this opposition and the Orange Order in general and Portadown in particular, saw a large influx of new members.

The 12 July 1887 saw the Portadown brethren walking the six miles to the demonstration field in Lurgan. *The Portadown and Lurgan News* dated 16 July reported at length on the proceedings which included a stirring speech against Gladstone and Home Rule by Colonel Saunderson, acting in his capacity as Deputy Grand Master. The Earl of Erne, the Irish Grand Master was also in attendance and the religious aspect of the service was conducted by the Dean of Armagh. The report began with a long discourse on the need for the Orange Order and the part the organisation had played in preventing the imposition of Home Rule as follows:

Once more the Orangemen all over the world have commemorated the battle of the Boyne and once more the enemies of civil and religious liberty have been shown what a great and increasing force Orangeism is in relation to the history of the United Kingdom ... the gatherings ... gave unmistakable proof that in their progress towards the dismemberment of the Empire, Mr. Gladstone and his colleagues will first have to sweep away hundreds of thousands of good men and true who are ready to do battle for the preservation of these principles which their forefathers safeguarded at Derry, Aughrim, Enniskillen and the Boyne.

The report then continued with a description of Portadown and Lurgan both of which had been well decorated for the occasion:

From an early hour on Tuesday morning the Orangemen of Portadown and Lurgan were astir, and the beating of the drums through the principal thoroughfares foretold the great enthusiasm which was to be displayed later in the day. The streets in almost every part of both towns were decorated with handsome arches, amongst the floral embellishments of which orange lilies formed a handsome portion... The sides and tops of the arches were covered with various coloured fabrics and crowns surmounted the structures flanked by flags. Some of the devices were – 'Derry', 'Aughrim', 'Boyne', 'Welcome Saunderson', 'Welcome Earl of Erne' and 'God Save the Queen'.

The newspaper concluded that 'never before has there been such a warm-hearted endeavour on the part of the loyalists of this locality to show their strength, their respectability and their devotion to the constitution'. Estimates of the number of Orangemen taking part were put at around 20,000 which in addition to the normal County Armagh Districts included contingents from Lower Iveagh (West) District LOL 8 with 21 lodges and Aghalee District LOL 21 with 7 lodges. Many of the brethren travelled by train but at the end of the proceedings the County Grand Master of Armagh commented that he hoped the Great Northern Railway would see fit to lower its rail fares for the next demonstration!

Portadown was the venue for the 12 July

celebrations of 1888 but it is not recorded whether the brethren travelling to the town were able to avail of cheaper rail fares.

The Bicentenary of the Battle of the Boyne 12 July 1890

Although the Home Rule Bill had been defeated by a narrow vote in the House of Commons, Charles Stewart Parnell and his Home Rule Party kept up the pressure with constant and unremitting agitation. By the beginning of the 1890s another Bill was in the offing by Gladstone's Liberal Party, waiting in the wings and heavily dependent on Irish votes. Meanwhile, Portadown Orangemen were as determined as ever to maintain their cherished position as citizens of the United Kingdom. One major event was to focus their attention on the need for unrelenting opposition to any future Home Rule Bill. That event was the Bicentenary of the Battle of the Boyne. Orangemen from all over Armagh and Tyrone converged on the market town of Dungannon to celebrate the glorious occasion and also to prepare for what lay ahead. The *Portadown and Lurgan News* reported at length on the monster gathering on 19 July 1890:

The Twelfth of July
Great Demonstration at Dungannon

The anniversary of the Battle of the Boyne , and the bicentenary of the landing of King William was celebrated in Portadown on Saturday last with undiminished enthusiasm. At ten o'clock the Orangemen of the District assembled at the Orange Hall, Carleton Street and half an hour later marched in procession to the Railway Station en route to Dungannon to participate in the great Orange demonstration which was held there and which was perhaps one of the largest and most enthusiastic gatherings of Loyal men held in the province of Ulster on the Twelfth.

The Earl of Ranfurly, who had kindly granted permission for the brethren to gather on his demesne, was unable to attend as he had just arrived home from Australia. Likewise the MP for North Armagh, Edward James Saunderson sent his apology for non attendance due to ill health. His let-

ter of apology was read and accepted by the Secretary of Portadown District Bro. R. Courtney. Nonetheless, in spite of the absence of these highly esteemed brethren, the proceedings proved to be a huge success. This was in no small measure due to the important contribution of many senior members of Portadown District LOL 1. The District Master of Portadown, The Rev. Andrew Leitch proposed the first resolution and this was seconded by the Rev. R. T. Simpson. Another member of Portadown District , Bro. W. H. Wright, proposed the second resolution. In seconding this motion, Bro. James Hamilton of Killyman District, made reference to this most auspicious of occasions and related how 'This part of the County of Tyrone and the adjoining County of Armagh was the birthplace of Orangeism and around the platform were assembled the descendants of those men who some ninety or ninety-two years ago formed the glorious Institution to which they had the honour of belonging'. Bro. Hamilton further alluded to the threat of Home Rule, the spectre of which, would hang over the Province in the event of a Liberal victory at the next election. That election victory came in 1892.

The Second Home Rule Bill 1893

With the shadow of the implication of Home Rule looming large the Orangemen of Portadown threw their weight behind their local MP Colonel Edward James Saunderson. In a famous speech delivered to the House of Commons he made the feeling of Unionists quite clear that on no account would they accept Home Rule under any circumstances. The House of Commons had already passed the Bill when later that year the County demonstration was held at Castledillon, the former home of the Molyneaux family. There was a large turnout of brethren from the County of the Diamond showing their opposition to Home Rule. The demonstration took place within sight of the imposing obelisk erected 'to commemorate the glorious revolution, which took place in favour of the constitution of the Kingdom, under the auspices of the volunteers of Ireland'.[2] The *Portadown News* dated 15 July 1893 reported on the demonstration thus:

The historic anniversary of the battle of the Boyne was celebrated in Portadown with all the enthusiasm of former years. The Orangemen of the district assembled at the Orange Hall in Carleton Street early in the morning and proceeded by train to Castledillon where a monster demonstration of the brethren of the county was held. During the day a number of country lodges and several bands paraded the streets playing the usual loyal airs.

There was a considerable police presence in the Obins Street area which had been the scene of serious rioting the previous year. On this occasion the Orange parade passed off peacefully which prompted the *Portadown News* to comment 'This speaks well for the members of the Orange Society, who have once more demonstrated their love for law and order'.

Two months later the Second Home Rule Bill was heavily defeated in its passage through the House of Lords. Ulster had once again been saved from Home Rule. However, the spectre would soon raise its ugly head once more in the early part of the twentieth century. Meanwhile, Orangeism grew steadily throughout Armagh and particularly in Portadown where a number of new lodges were formed.

Into the Twentieth Century
The next County demonstration to be held in Portadown was in 1896 and the town was again the venue two years later in 1898. In 1899 the small thriving industrial mill village of Bessbrook hosted its first ever County Twelfth demonstration. Around this time some brethren were setting off on the long journey by troopship to South Africa to take part in the Boer War.

The demonstration in 1900 was held in Armagh whilst that of the following year was held in Tandragee where Portadown brethren listened intently to the words of the Duke of Manchester, the owner of Tandragee Castle. Ashgrove on the Garvaghy Road, Portadown, was the location of the field for the 1903 County demonstration, an area which has now changed quite considerably over the intervening years.

The venues for the next three Twelfth demonstrations were Loughgall (1904); Richhill (1905); and Killylea (1906). Later that year the death occurred of that fine and dedicated servant of Ulster and the Orange cause, Colonel Edward James Saunderson, MP for North Armagh.

The Death of Col. Edward James Saunderson MP 1906
When Edward James Saunderson died in October 1906 he had represented North Armagh for twenty-one years at Westminster. He was a distinguished Ulsterman from Castle Saunderson, County Cavan, and an eminent parliamentarian who espoused the Unionist cause and defended it tooth and nail, both in Ireland and at the Palace of Westminster. The Colonel, who at one time commanded the 4th Battalion Royal Irish Fusiliers, was first introduced to Portadown by Bro. W. J. Locke who was the District Master of Portadown from 1891 until his death in 1905. During the 1885 election Saunderson became the 'darling of the Orangemen of Portadown'[3] and he remained so until his death twenty-one years later. Saunderson was well-liked and respected in Portadown for the no-nonsense forthright representation he gave his constituents at Westminster. He will be forever remembered in Portadown for his famous speech regarding the introduction of the Second Home Rule Bill of 1893 which included the following immortal words 'Home Rule may pass this House but it will never pass the Bridge at Portadown'!

Because of his popularity and for the considerable contribution he made to Unionism and to Orangeism a collection was started for the erection of a memorial statue which was to be unveiled in the heartland of his North Armagh constituency just four years after his death.

Unveiling of Col. Saunderson's Statue
The impressive memorial statue to the late Colonel Edward James Saunderson MP for North Armagh, was unveiled on 29 March 1910 in front of a huge crowd who had gathered in Market Square. Every available vantage point was taken, especially in the shops and offices that overlooked the town

centre. Adverts had been placed in the *Portadown News* offering seats in various establishments, one of which is reproduced below:

SAUNDERSON STATUE
UNVEILING CEREMONY
SEATS IN THE WINDOWS of the
extensive premises of Messrs. ROBERT
CORBETT & SON (directly opposite the
Statue)
TO BE LET FOR THE OCCASION
Proceeds to be devoted to charitable
Institutions
For terms apply
R. CORBETT & SON
Market Street, Portadown.

The town had been particularly well decorated for the occasion with bunting and flags festooned in every street of the town. A report in the *Portadown News* dated 2 April went 'Railway Street was ablaze with flags and streamers and the picturesque scene was continued along Bridge Street and High Street'. There was a large turnout of the brethren of Portadown District LOL 1 with every lodge having members on parade. *The Portadown News* reported:

Colonel Saunderson identified himself conspicuously with the Orange Order and the brethren turned out in their thousands to do honour to his memory. The members of Portadown district assembled at the Orange Hall and thence they proceeded to the railway station for the purpose of meeting the Belfast brethren who made the journey by special train.

They were joined by members from Lurgan, Armagh, Richhill, Tandragee, Dungannon and Orangemen from across the country. The impressive bronze statue of Colonel Saunderson was unveiled by Mr Walter Long in the presence of many distinguished guests who amongst others included: the Marquis of Londonderry, the Earl of Erne, the Bishop of Down and Connor, Dr Crozier and Colonel Robert H. Wallace. Amongst the many distinguished citizens of Portadown who were present were D. G. Shillington, Major and Mrs Stewart Blacker, Dr George

Dougan, David Rock and W. H. Wright, the District Master of Portadown.

From 1910 the bronze figure of Colonel Saunderson has been adorned with an orange sash on the 'Twelfth' of July in recognition of his abiding love for the Orange Institution and for the town of Portadown which he represented to the utmost of his considerable ability for many years.

12 July 1912

In 1911 the brethren of Portadown District travelled by train to Armagh for the 12 July demonstration whilst in 1912 they travelled the short distance to Tandragee. The peril of Home Rule was very much to the fore in the speeches delivered from the platform party. The newspaper commented on the growing strength of Orangeism in Portadown 'The growth of the Orange Institution in the Portadown District is remarkable, and during the past year its ranks have been added to by an unusually large number of new adherents'.

This increase in the numbers was due in no small measure to the fear of Home Rule and its consequences for the Protestants of Ulster. The following year the demonstration was held in Lurgan where Home Rule was once again denounced by all those present in the platform party.

The feelings against Home Rule and the opposition to it were soon marshalled into a well disciplined body created especially to prevent Home Rule being foisted on the people of Ulster against their will. That body eventually became known as the Ulster Volunteer Force.

**The Ulster Volunteer
Force in Portadown**

Major Stewart Blacker was the man who was chosen to raise and command the local contingent of what has become known as 'Carson's Army'. He had an impeccable war record behind him (he had served on the North-West Frontier and in South Africa) and was also a relative of Lt.-Col. William Blacker, the staunch supporter of the Orange cause, in years gone by. Many members of the UVF were members of the Orange Institution and in Portadown – the 'Orange Citadel' – the volunteer movement was dominated by local Orangemen. David Graham Shillington, and William Henry Wright, both of whom later became District Masters of Portadown District, were leading figures in the Ulster Volunteers at that time.

12 July 1914

As the 12 July 1914 beckoned tension was high on the European mainland with the assassination of Archduke Ferdinand of Austria in Sarajevo, a place still featured in the news bulletins today. By one of those quirks of history, an event hundreds of miles away and totally removed, from the politics of Home Rule, had a lasting effect on the shape of Irish history.

As the brethren of Portadown District gathered to celebrate the 12 July this far off event seemed, naturally enough, of little importance. 'We will not have Home Rule' were the words on everyone's lips. The 12 July in 1914 was held at Tynan, at the home of the Grand Master, James H. Stronge, a man whose family had served the cause of Orangeism for generations.

The Portadown brethren had set off from Carleton Street at 9.00 a.m. to parade to Edenderry from where they boarded the trains to Tynan. *The Portadown News*, dated 18 July 1914, commented on the decorations that had been erected in the town:

A great deal of time, and a considerable sum

of money had been expended in the decoration of the town... In the main streets were erected artistic arches bearing notices recalling the struggles of the past for faith and freedom, and the historic watchword of Derry's heroic defenders 'No Surrender'. As usual the arch erected in Edenderry attracted a great deal of attention... It was a splendid model of the gates of Derry, with the Mountjoy on one side and Roaring Meg on the other, surmounted by the motto, 'We will not have Home Rule'. Beautiful arches were also to be seen in Castle Street, Corcrain, Thomas Street, Carleton Street and many other thoroughfares.

The grounds around Tynan Abbey were swamped with the large influx of Orangemen and supporters who had travelled from all over the country. Estimates of the crowd were conservatively put at 10,000. Amongst those on the platform party were W. H. Wright, David Moore and David Rock – all high ranking officials from Portadown District.

The events on the European mainland seemed of little relevance. However, all this was to change and the course of Irish history altered, when on 4 August 1914 Britain, safeguarding Belgium's neutrality, declared war on the invading Germans. The Great War, a war that would cost the lives of over 400 men from Portadown, had begun.

VII

The World Wars

The Great War

HUNDREDS of Portadown Orangemen enlisted in the forces during the hostilities. Most joined the 9th Battalion Royal Irish Fusiliers, which was commanded by Lt.-Col. Stewart Blacker, the commander of the Ulster Volunteer Force in Portadown. Graham Shillington, later a District Master of Portadown District, became a major in the 9th Batt. RIF whilst Dr George Dougan, who was to succeed Bro. Shillington as District Master, gained a commission in the Royal Army Medical Corps.

Portadown brethren served in every theatre of the Great War, from the retreat from Mons to the carnage of Ypres and from the mud-soaked trenches of the Somme to the heat, sun and death of Gallipoli. Surprisingly, there is little or no mention of casualties amongst Orangemen in the District minute books. There seems to have been a convention not to mention or record the catastrophic losses being suffered by those at the front. As a result the names of many of those who served in the Forces, or who were killed, have not been recorded.

On the home front the first 12 July demonstration of the war was held at Moyallon. The *Portadown News* dated 15 July 1915, reported on the subdued atmosphere prevalent at the demonstration 'Owing to the general depression provided by the war, and the fact that large numbers of the brethren have joined the colours, the celebration was of a very simple character'.

The brethren were headed by the Salvation Army band, as they paraded to the field at Moyallon. There were no flags, banners, drums or fifes on display. The many speeches included one by a Portadown Orangeman, Sergeant-Major Robinson, who was serving with the Canadian Forces. He related how 86,000 Canadians had already joined the Colours of whom 34,000 were Or-angemen either directly, or indirectly, connected with Ulster.

The Battle of the Somme, 1916

The 12 July 1916 was to be like no other in the history of the Orange Institution. Only eleven days previously the manhood of Ulster had taken part in the Battle of the Somme where they had been killed in their thousands as they charged towards the German trenches. Soon after, the long casualty lists began to arrive in the town with almost every home having someone, a father, brother or son, killed or wounded at the Somme. It was a sad day in the history of Ulster. Many of those serving were, of course, Orangemen, who met, in lodge assembled, on the eve of the great battle. Some members wore their sashes over their uniforms as they went into battle.

As a consequence of the casualties amongst the 36th (Ulster) Division 12 July demonstrations were cancelled across the Province. Flags were flown at half-mast and blinds were drawn in nearly every household. Church services were arranged to pray for the wounded and the families of the fallen and to convey the sorrow felt at the grievous losses.

The *Portadown News*, dated 15 July 1916, reported on one such church service:

The 'Twelfth'

For the first time within the recollection of the oldest Orangeman in Portadown there was no demonstration in connection with the anniversary of the Battle of the Boyne, the lodges of the District complying with request of the Grand Lodge of Ireland that there should be no celebration this year... There was a large attendance, and the service was of a very solemn and impressive character. The flag of the empire and the flag of Ulster, draped in mourning, were displayed in a prominent position in front of the congregation... In the course of his address Canon Moeran paid a warm tribute to the soldiers of the Ulster Division who had fought so valiantly in defence of the flags.

At the end of the service a collection was taken up in aid of the UVF Patriotic Fund.

The 12 July demonstration of 1917 was held in a field in the townland of Drumgor, near Lurgan, which was kindly loaned for the occasion by Mrs Wells. Arches were erected in the town as usual, but the parade was smaller than before due to the number of Orangemen at the Front. The speakers made reference to the glorious attack of the 36th (Ulster) Division and to the threat of the imposition of Home Rule once peace was restored.

In 1918 the brethren returned to Moyallon where they listened to speeches again on Home Rule and on the possibility of the government introducing conscription to Ireland. By this time the British and Allied forces were beginning to take the upper hand against the Germans who were now in a state of exhaustion.

Four months later on 11 November 1918 an armistice was signed. The Great War, a war that would 'end all wars', was over. The first 12 July to take place in a now peaceful Europe was held at Carrickblacker, the home of Lt.-Col. Stewart Blacker DSO, late commander of the 9th Battalion RIF. At this historic meeting the colonel presented the regimental colours of the 9th Battalion to Portadown District LOL 1 in recognition of the large number of Orangemen who had served in the regiment during the war. In handing the flag over Blacker remarked that the flag should be kept for posterity 'as a loving remembrance of the old Battalion which so many members of the Order joined; a remembrance of those who had gone and an incentive to those who remain'.

One conflict had finally come to an end but another was about to begin. Already the Anglo-Irish War was raging in the South with the GOLI headquarters in Dublin coming under fire. For the next few years the embryonic state of Northern Ireland would come under serious assault from the IRA.

The Troubles of the 1920s

Portadown became the refuge for scores of Protestants in 1921 as republican violence and intimidation, in the aftermath of the setting up of the Irish Free State, reached its height. The Orange Order took a leading role in helping to resettle these families from the border counties of Cavan, Monaghan, Leitrim and other areas of the south, many of whom arrived in Portadown with only the clothes they wore. Many of these unfortunate refugees were Orange families, mainly from Cavan and Monaghan, and a number remained in the town, being helped by members of Portadown District to get houses and obtain employment.

A number of Orangemen from Portadown travelled to Cavan and other areas to help families pack their precious belongings and move house. These people, victims of ethnic cleansing long before the term was heard of, and whose only crime had been loyalty to the Crown and the Protestant religion, regarded Portadown as a place of refuge.

Bro. David Rock, District Commandant USC

Portadown earned the enviable reputation of being the largest town in Ireland to escape the worst horrors of 1920–22. While the rest of Ireland experienced murders, bombings and shootings, combined with rioting, the town of Portadown remained relatively unaffected. This situation was due in large measure to the dedicated efforts of leading Portadown Orangeman, David Rock.

Bro. Rock, who was renowned for his service to the Orange and Black Institutions was district commandant of the Ulster Special Constabulary in Portadown during the troubled years of the 1920s. It was his leadership, combined with the discipline and dedication of his men which maintained peace in the town.

There were only a few incidents in Portadown during the 1920–22 period – a remarkable state of affairs considering the state of anarchy that existed throughout most of Ireland at that time. One incident that caused intense feeling throughout the town was the brutal murder of a young Portadown Orangeman serving with the 'A'

Special Constabulary. Bro. William McKnight from Mary Street was mortally wounded in an IRA ambush in County Tyrone in 1922 and died a few days later. A popular member of Seagoe LOL 26, McKnight had served with distinction in the Great War with the Inniskillings and his murder caused a feeling of revulsion and outrage in Portadown. In spite of efforts to prevent retaliation a young Roman Catholic man was shot by gunmen a few miles from the town. There were real fears of rioting in Portadown, but prompt action by Bro. David Rock and the Specials maintained the peace.

Years later, when Joe Devlin, the MP for West Belfast, spoke at a nationalist function in Portadown he was eminently fair in paying tribute to the people of the town for their tolerance and good sense during this period. David Rock was one of the prime reasons for this and he was a man who commanded the admiration and respect of his fellow citizens, who elected him to the local Urban Council. Although Bro. Rock held office in his private lodge and preceptory – he was Worshipful Master of LOL 56 and RBP 503 – he did not attain the office of District Master. However, his influence was felt at all levels of Portadown District as well as throughout County Armagh. When David Rock died in October 1937, there was a huge attendance at his funeral and the brethren of Portadown subsequently erected a memorial headstone at his grave in St Saviour's Parish Churchyard, at The Dobbin.

The Women's Orange Association

During the 1920s there was an unprecedented expansion in the Women's Orange Association and although there were many reasons for this upsurge in popularity, the changing role of women in society, brought about by the Great War, would have been a major influence.

On 21 May 1921 the first Women's Orange Lodge WLOL 62 was founded in Portadown in Carleton Street Orange Hall. Sister Mrs Mary S. A. McDonald was installed as the first Mistress of the lodge. A year later, on 26 May 1922, a second Women's lodge, WLOL 85, was formed at Clounagh Orange Hall with Sister Mrs Jane Smyth being elected as Mistress. There then followed in quick succession the formation of several additional Women's lodges as the impetus and role of women increased, WLOL 101 was formed on 8 May 1923 at Edenderry with the first Mistress being Mrs Jessie Collen. WLOL 98 was formed a week later on 14 May 1923 and although this lodge was centred on the south Armagh village of Newtownhamilton it came under the jurisdiction of Portadown District. In March 1924 the last of the five lodges formed in the 1920s came into being when WLOL 109 was formed. These lodges in turn formed the Portadown District WLOL 3 and on 26 February 1927 the Armagh County Women's Grand Lodge came into being at a meeting in Carleton Street Orange Hall.

The 1920s also saw the formation of the first Junior LOL formed in the town when R. J. Magowan, the Worshipful Master of Edenderry LOL 322, instituted Edenderry Junior LOL 51 at Edenderry Orange Hall on 8 March 1927. The Juniors provided a steady flow of members into the senior ranks over the years and it wasn't too long before other senior lodges in the Portadown area began to form Junior lodges, notably Clounagh JLOL 45, Corcrain JLOL 120 and Parkmount JLOL 150.

12 July Demonstrations 1920–1927

The 1920 July demonstration took place in the townland of Ballylisk due to the opening of the new Orange hall erected by members of LOL 80, whilst in 1921 the brethren went to Loughgall. Derryhale was the venue for the County demonstration of 1922, again due to the opening of a new Orange hall which had been erected by members of LOL 81. In 1923 the brethren of County Armagh joined with their counterparts of County Down to attend the 12 July demonstration at Newry. The demonstration was held as a mark of respect to the Protestants murdered by the IRA at Altnaveigh. Venues for 12 July demonstrations for the years 1924–1927 were: 1924 – Armagh; 1925 – Richhill; 1926 – Tandragee; and 1927 – Portadown.

Twelfth of July, Portadown, 1928

In 1928 the County demonstration was to be held in Lurgan and the Portadown brethren assembled as usual at Carleton Street Orange Hall for their parade through the town to the railway station at Edenderry. However, this was to be no ordinary parade as already there was 'quite a stir in the town' about the presence of one of Ulster's greatest artists, Sir John Lavery. He had travelled to Portadown from Belfast on an early train and had set up his easel in rooms above the Classic Bar. During the day he sketched and painted the massed ranks of the Portadown Orange lodges as they made their way through the town to board the trains for Lurgan. It was not by mere chance that Sir John selected Portadown as the setting for his painting. Lavery knew his native Ulster intimately and although Belfast had its bigger procession he decided to come to Portadown with its unsurpassed association with Orangeism. Evidently Sir John had a tremendous time on that auspicious occasion as he was later to recollect in an unpublished diary:

I have seen many processions and exhibitions of intense feeling but nothing to quite equal the austere passion of the Twelfth in Portadown. The colour was more beautiful than anything I have seen in Morocco, black and orange predominating with every other colour except green adding to its beauty and the dozens of big drums beaten with canes by drummers whose lives seemed to depend on the noise they were able to make, their coats off, their shirt sleeves rolled up, their rists (sic) bleeding and a look in the eye that boded ill for any interference...[1]

In fact Sir John Lavery, at the age of 72, was witnessing his first ever Orange demonstration. In his famous painting Lavery managed to capture the solemn mood of the marchers as well as the associated pageantry of the men on horseback, the long line of banners and the group of Lambeg drummers. The painting entitled *Twelfth of July, Portadown 1928* was the automatic choice for the front cover of this book and is reproduced by kind permission of the Ulster Museum where the original is on display.

The 1930s

The 1930s was to be a decade that would go down in history as a period when, due to world socio-economic problems, countries and their populations would suffer hardship. A world recession, on a scale never before experienced, exacerbated the social evils of poor housing, poverty and health related conditions as the decade progressed and finally culminated with the world plummeting into war.

Orangeism continued to thrive with increases in membership, despite this backdrop of world affairs. Under the guidance of the District Master, Major D. G. Shillington DL, MP, and his District officers, Portadown District Lodge continued to prosper.

'Orangeism in Portadown District'

Being ever mindful of the importance of Portadown in the County of the Diamond and the influence of Portadown District in the early organisation of the Orange Order, a book was published in 1935. This publication, entitled *Orangeism in Portadown District* was written by W. H. Wolsey.

William Henry Wolsey was a local newspaper proprietor and a member of the Orange Order and the Royal Black Institution. Born in Newry, he moved to the Portadown area at an early age. A quiet, modest man who did not seek the limelight, he did, however, throughout his lifetime accumulate a massive amount of knowledge of the Orange Institution, not only in Portadown District but throughout Ireland. In his book he documented the history of the Orange Order in Portadown up to 1935. In his author's note he stated:

My object in compiling this History of Orangeism in Portadown District is primarily that of getting the Brethren of the District, and outside it, to take a keener interest in their Order and its principles, and to indicate a little of what difference there is between the so-called liberty our fathers knew and that to which we are accustomed today.

Without doubt W. H. Wolsey left for succeeding Orange brethren and historians a clearly documented record of the early formation and growth of Orangeism in Portadown, so much so that today his work is rec-

ognised as the foremost authority on the issue. Certainly, his book and additional arti-
cles that he wrote on Orange issues as a
journalist have provided sources of valuable
reference for those seeking information on
their lodges and warrants within Portadown District. As the then District Master,
Major D. G. Shillington, DL, MP wrote in
his foreword in the book 'Mr. Wolsey has
placed all those who have the interests of
the Orange Order at heart under a great
debt of gratitude'.

The sentiments of these words, written so
many years ago, are as relevant today as
they were in 1935 and the authors of this
current work have known the benefit of the
record of events left to us by Bro. Wolsey.

Orange Anniversary Church Services
In July 1936 over 600 Orangemen walked in
procession for the traditional Boyne Anniversary service to Drumcree Parish Church.
It is interesting to note that in the report of
the parade and the service that appeared in
the *Portadown News* of Saturday 18 July
1936 it records that the parade was led by
'Bros. Major D. G. Shillington D.L., M.P.
Dist. Master: D. Rock M.B.E. J.P., District
and County Grand Secretary: Dr. G.
Dougan, Dist. Treasurer and Walker
Whitten Asst. Dist. Secretary'.

The report does not include information
on accompanying bands. This was because
at the time bands did not accompany Portadown District on church parades. The addition of marching bands would not take place
until the 1950s.

The Orange Identity
Firmly Established
One of the clearly visible signs, each year,
that signals the approach of the 12 July is
the appearance of Orange arches. The 1930s
were to see a number of new arches appear
on the streets of Portadown for the first
time.

The Parkmount area has long had an Orange arch, originally situated at the junction of Victoria Terrace and Park Road but
later erected close to its present site at the
riverbridge facing Ulster Carpet Mills.

In 1936 the Jervis Street arch was
opened. The arch, bearing a miniature of

the gates of Derry was declared open by a
Mrs Stewart. Mr David Rock MBE, JP pre-
sided at the opening and as well as local
residents a party of Apprentice Boys of
Derry were present along with Edgarstown
Accordion Band and Portadown Pipe Band.

The following year, 1937, a further two
arches were in place in Portadown. The arch
at Corcrain, a sixty-foot span comprising of
three archways and situated at Corcrain
Orange Hall was opened on Friday 9 July.
The brethren of Portadown District together with a large contingent of junior
brethren had earlier assembled at
Edenderry and led by Corcrain Flute Band
paraded via the town centre to Corcrain.
Bro. David Rock MBE, JP and County
Grand Secretary presided at the opening
ceremony and the cutting of the ribbon to
declare the arch open was performed by a
Mrs Woods.

The following evening, Saturday 10 July,
the new arch at Edgarstown was unveiled.
This ceremony was performed by Major Rt.
Hon. D. G. Shillington DL, MP, District
Master, who had recently been appointed
Minister of Labour in the Northern Ireland
parliament.

The Edgarstown arch, fifty feet wide with
a height of almost thirty feet at its highest
point, comprised five arches and was situated at West Street. The arch was dedicated
to the memory of Lord Carson. It was
unique in its construction in that the Royal
Standard, national emblems and Orange
symbols were encased in glass and illumi-
nated. A hard-working committee had
overseen the design and construction of the
arch under the Chairmanship of Mr Alex
Moore, however, tribute was paid to the late
William Holland under whose guidance the
Arch Committee had been formed in August
1936. Mr Richard Johnston, secretary to the
Arch Committee, presented Major Shillington with an Irish blackthorn stick following
the ceremony. The present Edgarstown
arch, now erected at Margaret Street and
unveiled in 1991, comprises some of the
original adornments from the 1937 arch.

A new arch was erected at Carleton
Street for the Twelfth celebrations in 1939
but did not reappear after the war.

As well as the street arches, flags and

bunting that each year adorn areas of Orange culture there are few events that mean as much to individual lodges as the unfurling of a new banner. A number of unfurling ceremonies took place around Portadown at Kilmore, Diamond Grange, Ballylisk and Teaguy Lodges in 1938.

At Kilmore a new banner was unfurled by St Aidans True Blues LOL 35. The banner was carried to Greenfield House, the home of Mr and Mrs Moffett. Here, in the presence of the assembled brethren the banner was unfurled by Mrs Moffett and dedicated by Canon Johnston. The banner bore a painting of St Aidans, the Parish Church of Kilmore and also a painting of the burning of the martyrs, Ridley and Latimer. A unique circumstance at the proceedings was the presence of a descendant of Latimer, the Rev. W. J. Latimer BA, Ballycairn.

Another unfurling is worthy of note although it concerns the new banner of Grange Conquering Heroes LOL 118, Loughgall District. This banner was unfurled by the Portadown Deputy District Master, Bro. David Moore. Bro. Moore lived at the Grange, and it was at his home that the unfurling ceremony took place. He was one of the veteran Orangemen at the time in the County of the Diamond, having been an Orangeman for over fifty years.

Twelfth July Demonstrations

The year 1936 saw the County Twelfth demonstration take place at Richhill. That Twelfth saw a record attendance of brethren from Portadown District. Portadown was alive early on the Twelfth morning to the sound of Lambeg drums and pipes as the lodges of the District entered the town to assemble at Carleton Street Orange Hall. The town was bedecked with flags and bunting, with arches at Edenderry, Parkmount and the recent addition at Jervis Street. Other arches were evident at Baltylum, Derrykeevan, Cloncore and the Birches.

The lodges assembled at Carleton Street and made their way through the town centre to the railway station at Watson Street. The parade was headed by St Mark's Old Boys Band followed by the District officers. Bro. David Moore JP, Deputy District Master, travelled by car at the front of the parade. Other bands in the colourful procession included Parkmount Flute Band, Corcrain Flute Band, Seagoe CLB Pipe Band, Conn's Hill Accordion Band and Edgarstown Accordion Band. Following the journey to Richhill by train, the parade reassembled and, watched by thousands, made its way to the Field.

The day was reported in the *Portadown News* as a day when there was 'not a drop of rain' pleasing, no doubt, to the Lambeg drummers, and the only incident to mar the atmosphere was an accident to the County Grand Master, Sir William Allen DSO, DL, MP, as he arrived at the field. Although not seriously hurt he was advised not to take part in the speeches at the platform which resulted in Bro. George Crozier, the Deputy Grand Master overseeing the proceedings.

The Twelfth demonstration of 1937, the 247th Anniversary of the Battle of the Boyne, was held at Lurgan. Portadown District assembled in usual form at Carleton Street on the 12 July morning. Amongst their numbers included visiting brethren from Canada who had elected to join with Portadown District to enjoy the day. Derrycarne Pipe Band had the honour of leading the District and they were preceded by Bro. Tom Dermott on a decorated horse.

At the field the assembled gathering was addressed by the County Grand Master Bro. Sir William Allen. Visiting brethren from Canada and the Irish Free State were welcomed by the platform party. As well as the usual pledges of loyalty to the King and Constitution Major D. G. Shillington DL, MP, District Master of Portadown, made mention of the excitement felt by many on the impending visit, later in the month, of the King and Queen.

In 1938 Tandragee was to be host to the County Twelfth demonstration but by 1939 world events, that many had dreaded would occur, were imminent. Reservists were already being called up as Britain prepared for the outbreak of hostilities. The County demonstration took place in the small picturesque Co. Armagh mill village of Bessbrook and it was to be the last major gathering of Orange brethren for the duration of the Second World War.

Sir William Allen presided at the platform party over a large assembly of Orangemen. During his address Sir William launched a scathing attack on the British Government for abandoning the treaty Ports of Lough Swilly, Queenstown and Berehaven, bases which the Royal Navy could have used once war was declared. In the absence of the treaty ports Londonderry became a major naval base in the war against the U-boats.

Many of the brethren who paraded in Portadown and Bessbrook would soon be in the service of their country. Many would return following the war to parade as Orange brethren again, for others this would be their last Twelfth demonstration. The Sons of Ulster were prepared, for the second time, to demonstrate their allegiance to the Crown by fighting in its service those forces that sought to deny 'Civil and religious liberty'.

The Second World War

The ink was hardly dry on Chamberlain's famous piece of paper when Germany took over the Czech Republic in open violation of the Munich Treaty. A few months later, on 1 September 1939, Hitler's panzers rolled into Poland in a Blitzkrieg attack. Two days later Britain was, for the second time in twenty years, at war with Germany.

As in the Great War, although on a smaller scale, the men and women of Portadown District LOL 1 joined up in considerable numbers, throughout the six long years of war. They joined the Royal Air Force, the Army and the senior service, the Royal Navy. Many who were either too young, too old, or who were in reserved occupations, such as farming, enlisted in the Ulster Home Guard or enrolled in the Civil Defence organisations. Others also worked in factories supplying much needed war materials to the troops.

One Portadown Orangeman who took part in the war at sea was the late Bro. Joseph Henry of Portadown Ex-Servicemen's LOL 608. Stoker First Class Henry was a former employee of the Tavanagh Weaving factory before volunteering for the forces. In 1941 when on duty in the Mediterranean theatre, Joseph was lucky to escape with his life when the enemy bombed his ship. Later in the war his ship was torpedoed and sank with the loss of many lives. Edenderry man, Henry Kane, a veteran of the Great War and a faithful member of LOL 322 was lost at sea when his ship, HMS *Cape Howe*, was torpedoed by a German U-boat.

Bro. Henry Howard Maginn was one of a number of Portadown brethren serving with the Royal Air Force. He was a faithful member of Dr Kane's LOL 417, when he volunteered for service as an air gunner in Bomber Command. Sergeant Maginn was to lose his life on 11 September 1942 on a bombing mission over enemy territory. His body was brought home and he was buried in Seagoe Cemetery. Bro. David Gillis of LOL 127 was also to lose his life in action, whilst serving with the Royal Air Force.

Bro. Tommy Speers, a Past Master of Johnston's Royal Standard LOL 99, was part of a radar unit that went ashore in the early stages of the Normandy invasion. Resistance by the German defenders was heavy, as the D-Day veteran recalled in the *Portadown Times* dated 18 June 1994: 'There were 120 men in our radar unit and over half of them were killed or wounded. Most of them were very young and it is very sad to think of all those lives lost'. Bro Speers was given the honour of laying the wreath at the town's War Memorial during the District pre-Twelfth parade commemorating the 50th Anniversary of the D-Day landings. (Bro. Speers sadly died in November 1994, shortly after recording these events).

News from the Front was not always bad and from time to time Orangemen, who were serving in Irish regiments, were able to celebrate the anniversary of the Battle of the Boyne. Trooper Bobbie Rowland, a former outside left with Portadown Football Club, and then serving in North Africa with the North Irish Horse related how he and his comrades had celebrated the Twelfth in 1943. The report was carried in the *Portadown News* of 22 January 1944:

Portadown Men Had 'Wee Twelfth'

We had a bit of a night – an Orange one. There were about fourteen of us. There were two majors and a captain it was a great night! Well you can be sure the 'Sash' was heard all over the camp. The Portadown boys who were there were:– Jackie Day, James Crealey, David Black, Bob Fleming, Stanley McIlveen, a couple of boys from Armagh, a couple from Banbridge, one from Tandragee and one from Coleraine. They all voted it the best night they had spent since they joined the army. We had a 'Twelfth Night' and hope to have one later on.

During the war years in Portadown, as throughout the Province, there were no officially organised Orange parades. Carleton Street Orange Hall was requisitioned by the military and was used as a dormitory by officers of Welsh regiments stationed in the town. The District Lodge met in Edenderry Orange Hall. Major D. Shillington, himself a veteran of the Great War, was the Worshipful District Master of Portadown District, until his death in 1944, when he was succeeded by Dr George Dougan. One of his sons, Major Hampton Dougan, a holder of the Military Cross, died while on Active Service and the condolences of the District were conveyed to the Worshipful District Master at a meeting of the lodge on 24 January 1945. Similarly, sympathy was expressed to Bro. W. H. Wolsey on the death of his son, William, during the hostilities.

During the war years, despite the hardships at home and abroad, the Orange Order maintained its strength in the Portadown area. This strength was enhanced with the formation of a new lodge, Harmony LOL 500, in June 1944. This lodge, whose membership came mainly from the professional and business classes, took part in its first Orange procession in 1945.

The venue of the Twelfth of July in 1945 was Shamrock Park, with the main emphasis being on the great victory that the country had achieved over Nazi Germany. The celebrations were tinged with sadness as wives, children, brothers, sisters and parents remembered their loved ones who had been killed during the six long years of the war. Some brethren paraded wearing their service uniforms.

Amongst those from Portadown District LOL 1 who paid the Supreme Sacrifice during World War Two, the authors have identified the following brethren: Bro. James Taylor Tweedie (Army) LOL 19; Bro. John Gray (Civilian) LOL 56; Bro. David Gillis (RAF) LOL 127; Bro. Henry Kane (Royal Navy) LOL 322; and Bro. H. H. Maginn (RAF) LOL 417.

The *Portadown News*, dated 21 July 1945, made a fitting reference to these brethren who had made the Supreme Sacrifice in the defence of their country and who were noticeable by their absence from the 12 July Orange parade in their hometown:

The ranks of the Orange Order bore its 'honourable scars'. Many of the brave young lads who, six or seven years ago, had walked these selfsame streets, were no more and their absence from the Lodges or the bands was noticeable... Their valour, self-sacrifice and duty to King and Country were not forgotten, receiving special mention in the resolution submitted at the field. Some members who are still serving in the ranks were among those brethren who walked.

Some members of Portadown Orange District were still serving overseas and a small number of them were in action fighting the Japanese in the Far East. It would be another month before hostilities there came to a complete end, much to the relief of those soldiers, some of them Orangemen, languishing in the terrible conditions of the Japanese POW camps.

VIII

The Post-War Era

A Golden Age of Orangeism

THE period immediately after the end of the Second World War can easily be described as 'A Golden Age' of Portadown District LOL 1. There were many new and exciting opportunities on the horizon, new housing was being built and the town looked forward to a period of growth and prosperity. Among the Orangemen of Portadown District there was also a sense of optimism for the future and this was reflected in the large influx of new members. Men from the professional classes, including doctors, solicitors, ministers, teachers and businessmen associated closely with their working class brethren who worked in the town's factories. Indeed these professional men took a leading role in the development of Portadown District under the watchful eye of the Worshipful District Master, Dr George Dougan, the well known and respected General Practitioner.

This period was, arguably, the least troublesome time to have been an Orangeman in Portadown District and indeed throughout Ireland as a whole. At this time there was little or no hostility shown towards the Orange Order from any quarter whatever. The Order was regarded as a noble and honourable body whose aims reflected those of the Protestant community in general and as such gained a large measure of support from those outside the organisation. To be a member of the Orange Order, at this time, elevated a man in the sight of his peers. There was also no controversy over traditional parade routes. All parades in the town, including those through the 'Tunnel' passed off peacefully right up until the start of the 'Troubles' with no sizeable police presence needed to escort the marchers. Usually the total number of RUC officers present at Orange demonstrations amounted to one policeman at the front of the parade and one

to the rear. Due to the small number of cars and vehicles then on the roads, traffic control was not as yet a major problem. Finally, the civil strife brought about by the advent of the 'Troubles' in 1969, was still some way off. All these factors surely made this 'A Golden Age' of Orangeism.

The 12 July of 1946, the first after the complete end of hostilities of World War Two, was held in Lurgan whilst that of 1947 was held in Tandragee. In 1948 the brethren travelled to the small village of Poyntzpass which was famous for its Lundy celebrations on 1 July. District roll-call was at the rather late hour of 10.30 a.m., with the brethren parading to Edenderry to board the train for Poyntzpass. The return fair was 2s. 3d.

The cathedral city of Armagh was the setting for the County demonstration of 1949 and this was preceded by the usual 'Eleventh Night' celebrations as reported in the *Belfast Telegraph* 12 July:

Twelfth Eve
In Portadown
Revelling Until 5 AM

Fires were still smouldering in some districts in Portadown this morning after a night of general rejoicing at the approach of the 12. More bonfires than ever were lit in the town and at Parkmount the huge pile over which an effigy of Lundy had been placed was set alight by 85 year old Mr. Thomas McBroom – one of the borough's oldest Orangemen. Open air dancing and singing held the attention of the crowds till well into the morning and in one district it was nearly 5 o'clock before the last of the revellers had begun to move homewards.

Two years later preparations were well under way for the 12 July celebrations of 1951 with Portadown again the venue for the Armagh County demonstration. This was also Festival of Britain year and the town was particularly well decorated.

On 11 July 1951 Mrs Sarah Kane opened the new Edenderry arch. This was the fourth arch to be erected in the area, replacing the old wooden structure that dated from 1921.

A report in the *Portadown News* dated 14 July gives an insight into the tremendous feat of organisation that went into making the 12 July run smoothly:

Portadown Gets
Ready For Big
12th Celebration

Although weather conditions have so far been anything but conducive, preparations are going steadily ahead for the monster County Orange Demonstration. One hundred and twenty specially chartered buses will be in operation, while seven special trains are being run. In addition many others will arrive by car and other means of transport.

Already Portadown is bright with colour. In Market Street the Union Jack flies on the official Festival of Britain flagpole, and the first portion of miles of bunting to decorate the processional route has been erected.

In other parts of the town, too, the flags are out and the bunting is aloft. Arches have been erected at several points and altogether visitors to our borough should get a very favourable impression of the town on this important occasion.

In 1954 Portadown was again the venue for the Armagh demonstration, and there was a large number of new members on parade. One sad note, though, was the passing, in 1955, of the Worshipful District Master Bro. Dr George Dougan, who had contributed so much to the successful state that Portadown District was in. His successor, the popular Bro. R. J. Magowan of Edenderry LOL 322, carried on this good work and endeavoured to strengthen and even widen the influence of Orangeism in Portadown.

The Orangemen of Portadown used this period to further the religious aims of the Institution and this resulted in a large number of ministers joining some lodges within the District, most notably Wesleyan Temperance LOL 161 which had seven methodist ministers and Edenderry LOL 322, which had four from the Church of Ireland. Valuable time and resources also went into maintaining and consolidating the Orange presence in the area. Rebuilding and construction work was begun at many of the local Orange halls. In August 1954 a new hall was opened at Ahorey and in June 1956 Corcrain Orange Hall was reopened following extensive reconstruction. The Orangemen of Portadown District accompanied by bands and proudly carrying their colours paraded to the ceremony.

The Border Campaign

The reopening of this hall coincided with the launch of the IRA's so-called border campaign which lasted from 1956 to 1962. This period was characterised by attacks on RUC posts, Orange halls, villages and isolated areas all along the frontier with Eire, but especially in counties Tyrone, Londonderry and Fermanagh. During the County Armagh 12 July celebrations of 1957, which were held in Bessbrook, a squad of the Ulster Special Constabulary had to guard the railway viaduct in case of a sabotage attempt by members of the IRA.

Portadown was largely unaffected but when appeals were made by Orangemen for help in rebuilding halls damaged by the IRA the Portadown brethren did all they could to assist. One such appeal which received the attention of the District was from Anketell Moutray Memorial LOL 676 from Annahoe District in County Tyrone, whose hall had been demolished in an IRA bomb explosion. The hall was situated on the Favor Royal Estate just 100 yards from the border and at that time in use by the Favor Royal 'B' Specials. A three-man IRA unit ordered the caretaker and his little daughter out of the hall, at gunpoint, before planting the device. It was a portent of what was to come just a few years later.

Some Twelfth July Venues

In 1958 the Armagh County Twelfth demonstration was held in the city of Armagh.

Change was already occurring within the county at this time due to the downgrading of the railway system, which had operated so effectively for generations. For the first time Portadown Orangemen travelled the eleven miles to Armagh by bus. It took a fleet of 25 double-decker buses to convey the 1,500 Orangemen plus their families and supporters to take part in the demonstration at a cost of 4s. 6d. (22.5p) per person.

The 12 July 1961 saw the County demonstration held at Loughgall village, the historic birthplace of Orangeism in 1795. To specially mark the event, James Sloan's house, in which the first Orange warrants had been issued, was reopened as an Orange Museum. The opening ceremony was performed by Wor. Bro. R. J. Magowan OBE, JP, County Grand Master and District Master of Portadown District LOL 1. Through his contact with many brethren from all over the world, Bob Magowan had played a prominent role in the refurbishment of Sloan's house and the setting up of the museum.

Portadown hosted the County demonstration in 1962 and that year also saw the 50th Anniversary of the signing of the Solemn League and Covenant. Although no Grand Lodge of Ireland celebration took place in connection with this historic event, Belfast County Grand Lodge hosted a parade in the city to Balmoral Showgrounds, which was attended by many Orange brethren from Portadown.

Richhill was the setting for the 12 July demonstration of 1963 – the 273rd Anniversary of the Battle of the Boyne. The County Grand Master Bro. R. J. Magowan took the chair at the platform during the reading of the three resolutions. In that year thanks were expressed for the work of Lord Brookeborough who had stepped down as Prime Minister of Northern Ireland. He was succeeded by Captain Terence O'Neill.

R. J. Magowan, the District Master since 1955, passed away in 1968, a death that was lamented throughout Northern Ireland. Later that year Bro. Herbert Whitten was elected as the new District Master of Portadown District, a position he held until his death in 1981.

The Troubles

By the time Portadown District's turn came around again to host the Armagh County demonstration in 1971, the province had been plunged into the period now euphemistically known as the 'Troubles'. In this year the County parade made its way through the town centre of Portadown en route to the new field on the Loughgall Road, a departure from the previous venue of Shamrock Park. The field, situated near Kilmoriarty Orange Hall, was kindly loaned for the occasion by Bro. Herbert Whitten. During the customary speeches and the accompanying resolutions there was an unprecedented outbreak of heckling from a small section of the crowd, strategically placed quite close to the platform. Some were Orangemen, who were later suspended from the Institution for their unacceptable behaviour.

From the onset of the civil disturbances it had become apparent that there was growing resentment of traditional Orange parades passing through the Obins Street area of the town. There were clashes and confrontations between nationalists and the Security Forces mainly over the erection of barricades which were placed across the road in order to prevent the Orangemen from parading. This violence increased considerably in July 1972 when a concerted attempt was made to prevent Orange parades from entering the Obins Street area. Republican terrorists were orchestrating the violence which became quite severe in the run up to the July anniversaries.

In the early hours of 12 July 1972 an event took place that was to stun the whole community in Portadown. A 19-year-old Protestant youth, Paul Beattie, was found shot dead in an entry off Churchill Park. It was the town's first sectarian murder. Republican terrorists were known to have been responsible but the IRA never admitted carrying out this cold blooded act of murder on an innocent young man. Before the end of the day two other people, Jack McCabe and William Cochrane had been murdered in McCabe's Bar in High Street. Thus began a cycle of sectarian killings that was to result in a further four deaths by the end of 1972 and many more fatalities in the years to follow. Some of these victims were Orangemen.

The 1970s saw Portadown, like many other towns in Northern Ireland, suffer from the ravages of wanton terrorist attacks. The town was to receive its share of car bombings, incendiary attacks and shootings. The appearance of the town centre was to change considerably as many of the well known older buildings were destroyed and security gates, window grills and bollards were erected in an effort to thwart the terrorists. Intimidation became rife throughout many areas of the town as community relations deteriorated.

It was clear that to nationalists and republicans Orangeism was the complete antithesis of their ideological aspirations and was in fact the bedrock on which the Protestant and British people of Northern Ireland relied for direction and support. This hatred of the Orange Order and all it stood for manifested itself in the large number of purely sectarian attacks made upon the members and meeting places of the Institution.

On 17 August 1973, 36-year-old Trevor Holland, a member of LOL 273, was gunned down from a passing car as he was standing outside a cafe in West Street, Edgarstown. On 3 June 1975, Bro. Alfred Doyle, a member of LOL 7, was murdered along with two of his friends in South Armagh. In March 1976 Donald Traynor, a 28-year-old soldier, was killed when a booby trap bomb exploded at Ballygargan Orange Hall. The bomb had been planted by the IRA. One of the early victims of INLA terrorists was Robert Walker Whitten, the 73-year-old brother of the District Master, Herbert Whitten. Walker, as he was known, died three months after being shot in the town by INLA gunmen. He was a member of LOL 56. In one of the most brutal and cowardly attacks, the INLA murdered Salvation Army member James Wright when an under-car booby trap bomb exploded at his home in Corcrain. James Wright was a member of LOL 127.

Many other members of Portadown District LOL 1 were injured in the violence of the 'Troubles', some still bear the scars that almost cost them their lives. Some were members of the USC, RUC, RUCR or the UDR, whilst others were civilians who were attacked simply because they were Protestants. A few just happened to be caught up in the violence which was not of their own making.

Complementing these barbarous outrages on innocent members of the community were attacks on the Orange halls of the area, most notably Corcrain Orange Hall, situated at the interface of the mainly nationalist Obins Street. This building and the Orangemen and bandsmen who used it, was subjected to a succession of unwarranted attacks over the years. Sectarian or pro-republican slogans were often daubed on the walls and attempts were made to break into the building and to set fire to it and the furniture inside. Brethren attending meetings in the hall had their car tyres slashed or their car body work damaged in some form. Petrol and paint bombs were often thrown at the building in an attempt to deface it and the naming stones have often been the subject of attacks. The fact that Corcrain Orange Hall still stands today is a tribute to the tenacity and forbearance of the brethren of Corcrain LOL 339.

Very often acts of violence such as daubing slogans are excused as vandalism and the murders are too quickly forgotten, except by the families and loved ones left behind. The republican violence of the 'Troubles' however reveals the insidious nature of the IRA/INLA campaign to continually keep gnawing away at a section of the community in the hope that their capitulation will eventually be achieved. Evidence exists which supports the view that a deliberate programme of ethnic cleansing has been carried out against Protestants throughout the province, most especially along the border counties. It is regrettable that the Civil Rights movement and its aims of 1969 had to be hijacked and manipulated by those who sought to overthrow the democratic wishes of the vast majority of the people of Northern Ireland. In order to achieve this the terrorists set about depriving both sections of the community of the most basic civil right – the right to life itself.

As the bombing and murder campaign continued into the 1980s more families were bereaved of loved ones and more buildings were destroyed in the never-ending cycle of violence. In a purely sectarian attack, which could never be justified under any circumstances the IRA brutally murdered Sir Norman Stronge, the former Speaker of the Northern Ireland Parliament and his son James, in a gun and bomb attack at their home at Tynan Abbey near the border.

Throughout the 1970s and the 1980s intimidation continued, resulting in hundreds of Portadown families moving house, and the town becoming polarised to an extent it had never previously experienced.

By the time Portadown District's turn came around again to hold the County demonstration in 1982, the death had taken place of Bro. Herbert Whitten the District Master of Portadown Orangemen. His death, in December 1981, was deeply felt by the Orangemen not only of Portadown but of those throughout the County of the Diamond. The departure of Herbert Whitten left a void in the District and threatened to cast a shadow over the forthcoming July celebrations. In his place was elected Bro.

John Brownlee, a long serving member of Edenderry LOL 322.

Bro. Brownlee's first love was to the Junior Orange Association in which he served at both District and County level. He brought his own particular style of leadership to Portadown District, which saw him as a hard-working, diligent man with a great skill for organisation. Bro. Brownlee inherited an Orange District, which despite the 'Troubles', had been able to increase its membership considerably.

The 12 July parade in Portadown in 1982 was one of the largest for many years, with an impressive turnout of local brethren. Although there was the, by now, usual agitation over the traditional parades through the Obins Street area, everything passed off peacefully. No one on parade that day could have foreseen that events over the next few years, concerning the re-routing of traditional Orange parades, would culminate in probably two of the worst years in the history of Portadown District LOL 1.

IX

The Re-routing Controversy of 1985

THE re-routing controversy of 1985–86 was perhaps one of the most traumatic periods in the history of Orangeism in Portadown District. The town of Portadown was catapulted into the headlines of all the television news bulletins and the national newspapers, because of the serious public disorder that materialised as a consequence of the ban on traditional Orange parades. It was a situation that no one in Portadown District had wanted but one in which they were powerless to do anything about. A feeling persisted among some District officers that Portadown's situation was not sufficiently understood by sections of the Grand Orange Lodge of Ireland, which they considered could have done more to support Portadown District.

Only within the past few years has the District and the town recovered from those awful events and it is hoped that those violent scenes witnessed in 1985–86 will never return to the streets of Portadown.

This chapter and the proceeding one deals in depth with the whole re-routing controversy that affected Portadown Orangemen in the mid-1980s and contains the first full analysis of the reasons behind the re-routing and the violent aftermath that ensued. In order to understand the intricacies of how the re-routing of traditional Orange parades had such a profound effect on the Orangemen of Portadown District LOL 1 it is necessary to briefly examine the history and development of the town which in itself gave rise to the problem in 1985 and 1986.

Setting the Scene

The early origins of Portadown are unclear but the name is an anglicised corruption of the Gaelic *Port na Dun* or the 'landing place of the fort'. One early fort was the Lime Kiln fort near the Point of Whitecote. What is

known is that there were two religious settlements at Drumcree on the north-west side of the town and at Seagoe on the north-east. Both these areas would later be of a great significance to the members of the Orange Order. As the town grew from its humble origins as a Plantation settlement in the seventeenth century the first seeds that would later cause so much friction were being sown. Roman Catholics settled along the main road to Dungannon in an area which later became known as the 'Tunnel'. This small enclave was surrounded by farmland on three sides and by the growing town of Portadown on the other.

Due to its proximity to the site of the battle of the Diamond, Portadown was quick to embrace the ethos of Orangeism and throughout the nineteenth century played a prominent role in establishing and moulding the Order. The rebellion of 1641, although then only a folk memory, must certainly have encouraged participation in the fledgling Orange Order for Protestants saw it as a bulwark against any future repetition of the massacres of 1641. Portadown quickly assumed the title of the 'Orange Citadel' and throughout the British Isles, its loyalty to the Crown was unchallenged. As early as 1807 the first Orange parade made its way via what is now called Obins Street, to a church service at Drumcree, the site of an early religious settlement alluded to previously. It was of course at that time, the only available route that could be used and as such it became traditional for Orangemen to use it.

One of the earliest recorded incidents that occurred in the 'Tunnel' was in 1873 when Orangemen were attacked on their way home from a parade in Armagh as was detailed in Chapter V. The following year Orangemen from Lurgan were also attacked as they were leaving Portadown. This seems to have marked the end of this brief out-break of trouble. In the following year LOL 99 held lodge meetings in Obins Street so it is clear even from this period that the area was not an exclusively Roman Catholic one. There are also references to a Methodist Chapel in the 'Tunnel' one hundred years ago, probably a Primitive or Wesleyan Methodist building. As yet the 'Tunnel' area was still a small enclave but in later years more and more houses were built and many more people including Protestants went to live in the area.

The 1950s and '60s saw an increase in employment opportunities in Portadown and with it an increase in the need for im-proved housing. A programme of slum clear-ance began with the old housing in Curran Street, Mary Street and John Street being demolished to make way for new schemes. At that time the Upper Garvaghy Road was a country thoroughfare and was bounded mostly by fields and the site of the famous McGredy's rose nursery. New houses were built along the Garvaghy Road which ran parallel to Obins Street and which was separated from it by the People's Park. The first development in Lower Garvaghy Road was Woodside which was built just after the war and which housed mainly Protestant families. This was followed in the late '60s by Garvaghy Park, Churchill Park and fi-nally Ballyoran in the early 1970s. At first these housing estates housed tenants from both the Protestant and Roman Catholic communities, although the Garvaghy devel-opment, which backed onto Obins Street had a higher percentage of Roman Catho-lics. Lower Garvaghy Road – Parkmount – has always been a staunchly Protestant and Loyalist district with streets such as King Street, Victoria Terrace, Parkmount and, more recently, Woodside Estate.

The advent of the 'Troubles' soon had a serious effect on the religious balance of the housing estates along Garvaghy Road as Protestants were intimidated out of their homes in Garvaghy, Churchill and eventu-ally out of Ballyoran as well. Roman Catho-lics, who were forced out of their homes in Protestant areas, went to live in those houses vacated by Protestants. The sectar-ian divide in housing was becoming more

and more pronounced and this was to have serious repercussions for the traditional Or-ange parades. Where once Orangemen had walked along the Garvaghy Road to the gaze of no one, as there were just fields, they now walked past housing estates which were almost exclusively Roman Catholic and who resented the parade. These Roman Catholic estates now formed a crescent zone between the town centre and the outlying Protestant communities to-wards Dungannon and in particular Drumcree, with its Parish Church and Corcrain with its Orange hall. Together with Northway they remain as the only means of access to these areas.

During the 1970s and early 1980s re-peated attempts were made by the Roman Catholics of Obins Street and Garvaghy Road to prevent Orange parades from walk-ing through these districts. Barricades were constructed along the routes and running battles were fought with the police. Each time the RUC, backed up by the army, con-tained the trouble and allowed the tradi-tional Orange parades to pass through. However, as 1985 approached there were signs that this situation would not be al-lowed to continue and that the parade would not be allowed through the 'Tunnel' area. One of the best descriptions of this controversial area, written by Tim Cooke, appeared in the *Belfast Telegraph* of 5 July 1985:

The Tunnel itself is little to write home about. Turning off the main High Street, Market Street shopping area into Woodhouse Street you eventually encounter a 20ft long, 9ft high subway which allows pedestrians to pass under the busy Northway road. After 30 yards of open sky, passing the train station entrance, its under the railway bridge and into Obins Street which leads in turn to the bottom of the Dungannon Road. The end of Obins Street nearest the town centre is rather run down. Some of the terrace houses are lying open and derelict and many others are bricked up.

It was this run down area with seventy occupied houses and flats facing onto the street that the Eire government wanted declared out of bounds to the Orangemen of Portadown. They were insistent on proof from the British government that they were prepared to face down Unionist opposition to the forthcoming Anglo-Irish Agreement. Where else could the government choose as a symbol of loyalist Ulster, than Portadown, the 'Orange Citadel'.

The Events of 1985

One of the first signs of impending friction appeared in March when the RUC stopped a Roman Catholic accordion band from marching along Park Road and Parkmount and past the predominantly Protestant Woodside Hill housing estate. The band had returned from a St Patrick's Day parade in Cookstown. Following a day of tension in the area, nationalists stated their intent to organise counter-demonstrations in July to prevent Orange parades from using their traditional route through Obins Street. SDLP Senator, Mrs Brid Rogers was quoted in the *Irish News,* dated 18 March 1985, as saying, the re-routing of St Patrick's Accordion Band 'was in stark contrast to the RUC's attitude every July when large contingents of police forced a loyalist parade through the hundred percent nationalist Obins Street area'.

During the intervening months pressure mounted to have Orange parades re-routed from the Obins Street area of Portadown. The Anglo-Irish talks at the time gave special importance to the re-routing issue, causing much concern amongst loyalists in general and the Orangemen of Portadown in particular. By June 1985 bans had already been imposed on band parades in Cookstown and Castlewellan which resulted in confrontations between the police and bandsmen. Unionist politicians made representations to the then Secretary of State, Douglas Hurd, regarding the forthcoming July Anniversary parades in Portadown. It was felt that as these parades were traditional and were well organised in a dignified manner, so as not to cause offence to anyone, that they should be allowed to proceed. The authorities, however, had other ideas.

By early July speculation was rife as to whether the Portadown parades would be re-routed in part, or completely banned, over the July period. To resist any such changes a monster rally of Orangemen, organised by the Parade Action Committee, was held in Portadown on 3 July. Its purpose was twofold, firstly to show opposition to the re-routing of traditional Orange parades and secondly to show the authorities that Orangemen could organise thousands of men in a dignified and orderly fashion. Orangemen from all over the province attended the rally. Clearly the re-routing issue was on everyone's minds.

Contact and consultation between officials of the Orange Order, Unionist leaders, the police and the Northern Ireland Office continued, amid growing speculation about the eventual outcome of such negotiations. At Westminster, Prime Minister Margaret Thatcher supported Mr Hurd's insistence that policing in Northern Ireland should be evenhanded. She stated that she would also back any decision made by the Chief Constable, Sir John Hermon, regarding the re-routing of Orange parades in Portadown. It was also reported, however, that the government had been careful to draw a distinction between 'support in principle' and any accusations that it was in any way forcing a change of parade route on the organisers.

By 6 July, the controversial decisions had been made and announced. The RUC had given the go-ahead for the Sunday Church parade to Drumcree, but had imposed a ban on entry to the 'Tunnel' on either the Twelfth or Thirteenth of July. In its article under the banner headline 'Sunday Parade Given Go-Ahead' the *Belfast Telegraph* reported a difference of opinion within the Orange Order. The Grand Secretary, Bro. Walter Williams, was reported as saying the Orange Order would abide by the re-routing on the Twelfth and Thirteenth of July, whereas Bro. Alan Wright of the Parade Action Committee called the re-routing 'unacceptable'.

On 7 July the Boyne Anniversary church parade organised by Portadown District LOL 1 proceeded, as it had done since 1807, via its traditional route of Obins Street to Drumcree Parish Church. It was later reported that up to 2,000 Orangemen took part in the parade which was led by officers of Portadown District LOL 1, accompanied

Perhaps the earliest photograph of an Orange Lodge in Portadown District featuring members of The Prince of Wales LOL 56 circa 1870s. (Courtesy: Portadown District LOL 1.)

The opening of Carleton Street Orange Hall, 12 August 1875. (Courtesy: Portadown District LOL 1.)

Members of Sir Edward Wingfield Verner's True Blues LOL 107, 12 July 1895. (Courtesy: LOL 107.)

Kane's Crimson Star LOL 417. This photograph was taken between 1896 and 1900, possibly at the unfurling of a new banner. (Courtesy: William Lavery.)

Colonel Edward James Saunderson (1837–1906) leader of the Irish Unionist Party, MP for North Armagh and prominent Orangeman. The Colonel's portrait is featured on the bannerette of LOL 58. (Courtesy: Albert Nicholl.)

Members of The Prince of Wales LOL 56 parading down Market Street, Portadown, prior to World War One. (Courtesy: Portadown District LOL 1.)

King William's Defenders LOL 127. This photograph dates from around 1918. Note the painting of Lord Kitchener (killed in 1916) on one of the Lambeg drums. (Courtesy: S. Thompson.)

Edenderry Temperance and Benefit LOL 322, circa 1920. (Courtesy: LOL 322.)

Edenderry Arch opened in 1921 and guarded by vigilantes raised by Bro. David Rock. (Courtesy: David Allen.)

Portadown Lambeg Drumming Club, 1927. (Courtesy: *The Portadown Times*.)

LOL 31 parading through Edenderry *en route* to the railway station, 12 July 1933. (Courtesy: LOL 31.)

Bro. T. Dermott of LOL 18 on white horse in Watson Street, 1937. (Courtesy: Portadown District LOL 1.)

Edgarstown Orange Arch. This photograph was taken in the early 1930s before the erection of a new arch in 1937. (Courtesy: R. Tedford.)

Corcrain Orange Arch erected 9 July 1937. Blown down in the mid-1940s the arch was never re-erected. (Courtesy: T. Lyttle.)

Major David Graham Shillington, DL, MP, Worshipful District Master
of Portadown from 1926 until his death in 1944. (Courtesy: LOL 322.)

Mrs Sarah Kane opening Edenderry Arch, 11 July 1951. Also featured are prominent local Orange personalities: Dr George Dougan, H. Whitten, W. H. Wolsey and Rev. J. W. Appelbe. (Courtesy: Vera Gallery.)

Robert Magowan OBE, JP, County Grand Master of A'magh and WDM of Portadown 1955–68 opening the Orange Museum, Sloan's House, Loughgall, 1961. (Courtesy: LOL 322.)

Drumheriff Star of Erin LOL 8 parading in Portadown 12 July 1962. (Courtesy: T. Houston.)

The Rising Sons of Portadown LOL 273, Inaugural Meeting 5 November 1969. (Courtesy: LOL 273.)

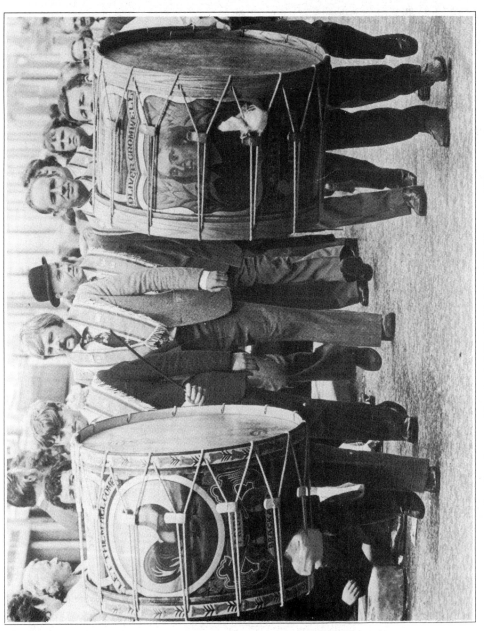

Lambeg drums of Brackagh LOL 18, 12 July 1973. (Courtesy: T. Houston.)

The late Bro. Herbert Whitten, JP, MP, Worshipful District Master of Portadown from 1968 until his death in 1981. LOL 40 was renamed in his memory. (Courtesy: Albert Nicholl.)

Members of King William's Defenders LOL 127 photographed under Parkmount Orange Arch, 12 July 1985. (Courtesy: S. Thompson.)

Crowds gather to protest at the re-routing of Orange parades away from Obins Street, 12 July 1985.

Portadown town centre on the evening of 12 July 1985.

The banner of Johnston's Royal Standard LOL 99 depicts the Drowning
of the Protestants in the River Bann, 1641. (Courtesy: Albert Nicholl.)

Part of the re-enactment of the Drowning of the Protestants at the River Bann commemorating the 350th Anniversary of the massacre. June 1991. (Courtesy: *The Portadown Times*.)

Portadown District LOL No. 1, Officers and Committee 1991–92. (Courtesy: Portadown District LOL 1.)

Drumcree Parish Church is featured on the banner of LOL 13. The church has hosted an annual church service since 1807. (Courtesy: Albert Nicholl.)

Drumcree Sunday, 9 July 1995. View from behind police lines.

Scene at Drumcree Parish Church on the evening of 10 July 1995 following
the large demonstration in support of Portadown Orangemen.

Portadown District LOL 1 makes its way along the Garvaghy Road on the morning of 11 July 1995, almost 48 hours after setting off for the annual church service.

Bro. Harold Gracey, Worshipful District Master of Portadown since 1986. (Courtesy: Albert Nicholl.)

by the colour party of Portadown Ex-Serv-icemen's LOL 608, and Bro. Harold McCusker MP and Bro. Martin Smyth, MP, Grand Master of the Grand Orange Lodge of Ireland. Prior to the entry of the parade to Obins Street, some trouble flared between protesters and the police. Following heated exchanges, two local Jesuit priests held discussions with the RUC, to allow a peaceful protest to take place. The following day the *Irish News* reported:

> Around 600 RUC men and dozens of Land Rovers were positioned to form a barrier between the nationalists and the Orangemen.
>
> Insults were hurled by the protesters, but there was no violence, as the three bands passed on their way to Drumcree Church in less than ten minutes.

The Twelfth of July 1985

The Sunday parade had passed off relatively peacefully, although, the controversial re-routing of the Twelfth parades was the main topic of conversation on all Orangemen's lips. At first local Orangemen made a call to their brethren in other districts to converge on Portadown on the 12 July to show solidarity with the plight of Portadown District. Following talks between leading members of the Orange and Black Institutions, the local RUC commander and the Orange Lodges' Action Committee, it was announced that local Orangemen would attend the County demonstration in Tandragee as planned.

This plan however did not materialise. What had been originally designed as an orderly protest against the re-routing decision soon turned into violent confrontations at the junction of Corcrain and Obins Street in the morning and later in the day at Woodhouse Street. A number of policemen and loyalists were injured in the clashes and eighteen protesters were arrested. Throughout the day repeated baton charges were made by riot police and a number of plastic bullets was fired in an indiscriminate fashion. Many windows were broken in Market Street as the town centre of Portadown was turned into a virtual field of battle between the police and loyalists

The riot police involved in this incident as in most of the controversial street scenes in

1985–86 were members of the Divisional Mobile Support Units – a quick reaction police unit trained in riot tactics.

The SDLP MP, Seamus Mallon was in Obins Street during the day and called upon loyalist leaders to give what he termed 'proper leadership'. When asked about Dublin's involvement in the decision to re-route Orange parades, the *Irish News* quoted him as saying 'I would be very disappointed if they had not made representations'. Seamus Mallon was reportedly accompanied on his visit to Portadown by Mrs Eunice Schriver, the sister of Senator Edward Kennedy. Unionist councillors on the scene roundly condemned the actions of the police and accused them of 'animalistic behaviour' against the Orangemen of Portadown District. Residents of Obins Street were kept under virtual siege for two days, by the police and the army who had blocked off all entrances to the area. Under normal circumstances in previous years the Orange parade took less than ten minutes to pass!

The following day, the Thirteenth of July, saw a continuation of the violence, only this time the trouble was confined to the main area of the town, at the junction of Market street with Woodhouse Street. Here demonstrators continued running battles with the police in the morning and in the evening, following the return of the members of the Royal Black Institution from Scarva. Those involved in the serious rioting were not members of the Black Institution but used the cover of the RBP banners and the parade to attack the police.

The effects of these trouble filled days were to reverberate throughout the entire community for some time. The RUC stated its commitment to remain in the Obins Street area following a vow by the Democratic Unionist Party that loyalists would march through the area once the police had left. Press Officer, Mr Sammy Wilson, was reported in the *Irish News* as saying that 'loyalists should not feel ashamed of confronting policemen who bowed to the demands of Dublin'. Republicans and especially Sinn Fein did not feel ingratiated towards the police either. In the same article referred to above, Danny Morrison said 'The major function of the RUC is to defend partition and no one should be fooled by such cosmetic gestures of alleged impartial policing'.

In the aftermath of the troubled July parades more than fifty individuals were charged with various Public Order offences, the hearings being held at Craigavon Magistrates' Court. Representatives of three local community associations met with senior RUC officers to discuss allegations of police 'brutality and over-reaction' towards the loyalist community in the town.

The Anglo-Irish Agreement
In November 1985 the worst fears of the Unionist population were realised by the signing of the Anglo-Irish Agreement, by the Prime Minister, Margaret Thatcher and the Irish Prime Minister, Garret Fitzgerald, at Hillsborough. The agreement gave the Eire government a role in the internal affairs of Northern Ireland, against the expressed wishes of the vast majority of the populace. Democracy, it seemed had been stood on its head. The elected representatives of the Unionist majority were totally excluded from any of the discussions. The Orange Order was instrumental in organising a mass protest rally which was held outside the City Hall, Belfast just one week afterwards. Official figures released by the RUC gave an estimate of the crowd at well over 200,000, the largest political demonstration ever held in the United Kingdom, even surpassing the large numbers that gathered to sign the Covenant on Ulster Day, 28 September 1912. Hundreds of brethren from Portadown District attended the parade and rally, travelling by train to their destination.

This mass protest and the total opposition to Dublin interference in Ulster had no effect on either the British or Irish governments. They carried on with their plans regardless of the democratically expressed will of the people. In fact government civil servants looked upon the protest as allowing the Unionist community opportunity to 'let off steam'. The situation did not auger well for the Orange Order in Portadown, faced as they were with the problem of Obins Street and the insistence of the Eire government that no parades should be allowed through the area.

X

The Crisis Deepens in 1986

AS the end of the year approached, talks had already been taking place between Orange leaders and the Chief Constable, Sir John Hermon, concerning the July parades in Portadown in 1986. Bro. Walter Williams, GOLI Grand Secretary, was reported in the *Irish News* of 5 December 1985 as saying 'I can't see at this stage Sir John changing his mind, but that is only a personal thought. We will have to wait and hear the result of the discussions with the new Portadown officers and the local divisional commander. It remains very doubtful if the parade will get through'.

The 1986 Apprentice Boys Parade

Despite the high level talks that had already taken place between Orangemen and the police the position did not improve as the new year began. In fact, the situation was further complicated by the Apprentice Boys of Derry who declared their intention to hold their Easter Monday parade in Portadown. Part of the proposed route included the Garvaghy Road area of the town. The parade was eventually banned at the last minute by the Chief Constable, Sir John Hermon. That ban was to have severe repercussions in the town over the next 24 hours. The RUC stated, amongst other reasons, that they had banned the parade because there was **no tradition** of an Easter Apprentice Boys parade in Portadown. It mattered little that the Orange parades in the town *were* traditional, but had been banned anyway. The police considered that 'paramilitary elements' would infiltrate the parade in an attempt to cause widespread serious disorder.

That night as news of the ban began to spread large numbers of the people of Portadown gathered in the town centre angered at the Chief Constable's decision. The Portadown Defenders Flute Band paraded around the town as more and more people, alerted by the music, came into the town centre. The parade made its way down Garvaghy Road to keep its route open and to defy the ban. Thousands of ordinary men and women from the town proceeded to walk through a small police cordon on the Garvaghy Road. As they did so the police informed the crowd that the parade was illegal. Some stones and bottles were hurled by youths from Churchill Park, but the spontaneously arranged parade continued peacefully along Garvaghy Road via Charles Street to the town centre.

By morning the town had been virtually sealed off by the RUC but this did not prevent some members of the Apprentice Boys from getting through the cordons. Reaction to the ban was bitter. Unionist politicians accused the RUC and the NIO of 'bowing to the dictates of Peter Barry and his republican friends in the Province'. They further contrasted the banning of the parade with the 'softly, softly' treatment of republican and IRA parades in the country. The *News Letter* reported that the ban had angered many RUC officers and quoted one as saying that the force's leaders had 'completely lost their heads'.

A parade did eventually get under way in Portadown. Conflict inevitably erupted, with the RUC firing an unprecedented number of plastic baton rounds – in the region of 150. As evening closed on the events of 31 March 1986, a Protestant youth, Keith White from Lurgan, lay in hospital, suffering from the effects of a serious head wound inflicted by a plastic bullet. He later died from his injuries.

The Drumcree Church Parade
6 July 1986

The approaching July parades threatened further violence in a town still recovering from the ultimately tragic events of Easter Monday. The months of June and early July saw repeated calls for the County Armagh Twelfth venue to be switched to Portadown to show solidarity to the brethren in the area. Chief among the supporters for this action was Bro. Harold McCusker MP. However, despite these calls from him and other influential figures, the Orange hierarchy set about dissuading the Portadown Orangemen from taking this course of action.

Early July saw Sinn Fein and other nationalists threatening protests against the traditional Orange parades. Protestant Church leaders including the Church of Ireland Primate, Dr Robin Eames; Presbyterian Moderator, Dr John Thompson and Methodist President, the Reverend Sydney Frame, urged the Orangemen to avoid confrontation, but added in their statement that they 'supported the right of all to have traditional peaceful marches and demonstrations'.

By 4 July the RUC decision on the parades issue had been made public. The Twelfth parade and the Royal Black Institution parade to be held on the 14 July (the 13 July was a Sunday) would be re-routed away from the nationalist Obins Street area. The Drumcree church parade was however given the go-ahead but only if stringent conditions laid down by the RUC were adhered to. A spokesman for the RUC said that their decision to allow the Orange parade to go through the nationalist area was dependent on it being 'a dignified, peaceful parade and on the tradition of respect accorded to church parades by the Roman Catholic community'. At the same time the RUC banned a proposed parade organised by a nationalist band, which had been deliberately timed to coincide with the Orange one. It was banned on the grounds that it was **not traditional** and was 'clearly designed to cause difficulties'. The RUC's attempt at compromise satisfied no one. The decision to ban the nationalist band from parading was later reversed, although the RUC stated that they could only parade at 3.00 p.m., long after the Orangemen had passed. The organisers maintained that the band would parade at 10.00 a.m. as planned.

The residents of Obins Street issued a statement, which, as well as attacking the Orange Order, for holding the church service, also attacked the RUC for allowing it to go ahead. The statement further attacked the Anglo-Irish Agreement as 'not being worth the paper it is written on'. As tension increased the Drumcree Faith and Justice Group gave notice that they would be holding a tea party on the Garvaghy Road. A spokeswoman added that the Orange church parade was 'an insult to the residents of the area'.

As the Orange parade entered the Obins Street on the morning of Sunday 6 July, it was confronted by a cordon of DMSU police wearing full riot gear. The police began pushing the marchers through the cordon in twos as they attempted to pick out certain Orangemen, brethren from other parts of the Province, who had a high political profile, whom they considered should not be permitted to walk through the 'Tunnel' area. Scuffles inevitably broke out as the tension began to mount in the confined space of the subway leading to the tunnel. Following a long delay the parade was allowed to continue on its way amid jeers and name calling from the local residents.

After the service at Drumcree the Orangemen prepared to walk along the Garvaghy Road on the return leg of their journey. A large number of policemen, with army support, were positioned along the route to prevent any clashes. Nevertheless, a protest was made by the People Against Injustice Group at the entrance to Garvaghy Park. Protesters ran onto the road in an attempt to block the path of the Orangemen, however the police quickly moved in to remove them. As the Orangemen proceeded on their way they were taunted by sectarian outbursts by the onlookers. Verbal abuse was hurled and many physical attacks were made on the dignified parade. Even though they had come under severe provocation, the Portadown Orangemen continued on their way without breaking ranks.

Condemnation of the events in Portadown came not surprisingly from both sides of the political divide. Mrs Rodgers of the SDLP was quoted in the *Irish News* as saying 'It is simply intolerable that the nationalist population of Portadown should be held prisoners in their own homes for most of the day in order to allow a totally unnecessary exercise in coat trailing and deliberate provocation by loyalists'. On the other hand, in the same article, former Councillor, Bro. Arnold Hatch, accused the RUC of 'deliberately provoking' the situation. The RUC issued their own version of events as follows:

The events in Portadown today speak for themselves. An opportunity was presented to the organisers to have a dignified peaceful parade. Regrettably this was not the outcome. Even before the parade got underway three police officers were assaulted and subsequently police were verbally and physically abused by participants and supporters.

At one point there was an insistence that a known troublemaker not from Portadown should take part in the parade contrary to prior conditions laid down by the police. His participation was not permitted by the police. During this altercation a number of officers were injured. Later a police Land Rover was overturned by persons wearing regalia in the vicinity of the church service and several officers were injured.

On the outward and return journeys police action prevented sectarian clashes and interference with the parade. At least 13 police officers were injured, including one hit in the neck by a dart thrown from a nationalist crowd.

An organised protest against the parade which took place at Garvaghy Road passed off peacefully. Overall four arrests were made, three of them loyalists. Others have been identified for report with a view to prosecution.

The statement was quite liberal in its interpretation of the facts. A spokesman for Portadown District denied any arrangement had been made with police regarding the barring of any individuals from taking part in the parade. It would have been contrary to the rules of the Institution to prevent a bona fide Orangeman from walking in a procession. The Orangemen of Portadown had already made a number of concessions to the police, through the years regarding the church parade. Only hymns were played by the bands and they had stopped playing completely when passing the Roman Catholic chapel. The unfortunate incident of the overturned Land Rover occurred, it was recalled, because in the midst of what was a highly volatile situation a policeman had stepped over the parameters of his professionalism by seeking to taunt Orangemen by use of a physically obscene gesture.

The 12 July 1986

On the 12 July the 32 lodges, comprising the 1,500 Orangemen of Portadown District joined with the other brethren of the County of the Diamond at the demonstration in Armagh. Despite calls for all Orangemen to converge on Portadown on the 12 July to protest at the re-routing issue, the advice from Orange leaders at Grand Lodge, was for lodges to attend their previously arranged demonstrations. Tension in Portadown on the 12 July morning was electric, however, a last minute compromise agreement was reached behind the scenes which enabled Portadown District to travel to Armagh.

The agreement hammered out was that the eight country lodges that formally paraded through the 'Tunnel' would walk along the Garvaghy Road on their way to the assembly point at Carleton Street Orange Hall. The police had carefully studied both routes and had determined that although there were three Roman Catholic housing estates bordering the Garvaghy Road, very few houses directly opened out onto that road. In the Obins Street area they had counted over 70 houses directly fronting onto the street. The police also considered that the Garvaghy Road was a major thoroughfare which anyone had the right to transverse, whereas Obins Street was a definite self-contained nationalist area. To avoid confrontation and to help develop the situation, the Orangemen agreed to this compromise, whilst still maintaining their preference for the traditional route of Obins Street.

Although the Portadown Orangemen had

enjoyed their day in Armagh there was much apprehension about the situation awaiting them when they returned to the town. The situation was not helped when a hitch in the transport arrangements delayed their arrival until 7.00 p.m. Crowds had been gathering in the town from mid-afternoon and the delay added to the tension already prevalent in the air. Bottles and stones were thrown at the police guarding the entrance to Woodhouse Street. The Orangemen were caught up in the riot, but did not break ranks. After a token protest at the police lines the parade moved off towards Carleton Street. As the parade made its way through the town, DMSU Land Rovers sped into the town from the direction of William Street, where they had been defending the chapel against an imaginary threat. The appearance of the Land Rovers in such a provocative manner made the situation worse and the crowd began to stone the vehicles as they passed Wellworths. At one stage a Land Rover was overturned and set on fire.

Extra riot police were drafted into the town and they formed two cordons across the street and began a clearance sweep. As the last of the lodges broke up in Carleton Street a line of riot police, complete with batons, shields, helmets, body armour and baton guns, appeared at Church Street in pursuit of a number of youths. A plastic bullet was fired indiscriminately into Carleton Street, resulting in the wounding of a totally innocent bystander. This sorry episode in police/Unionist relations was arguably the first time that the Unionist people in Portadown had been confronted in their own town centre by the totally alien sight of a police riot. The situation did not augur well for the Royal Black Institution's demonstration in two days' time.

The Events of 14 July 1986

During the early hours of the 13 July feverish activity was underway at the top of Woodhouse Street. Daylight revealed that army engineers were building a 12 feet high metal screen across the entrance. This marked a change of tactics by the police who could now hide behind the screen and not be seen from the town centre. The townsfolk thought it was tantamount to a part of the Berlin Wall erected in their midst. Shop owners in Woodhouse Street also complained that the screen affected their business, but the complaints were ignored.

The morning parade, on 14 July, by members of the Royal Black Institution, made a token protest at the screen before continuing to Scarva. This token protest was seen as inadequate by the large mob which gathered and who throughout the day tried to destroy the obstacle. An attempt was even made to drive a hijacked bus through the barrier.

In the evening as the Royal Black Institution parade made another protest at the barrier, the mob used the cover of the banners and marchers to throw missiles at the police in Woodhouse Street. Again massed ranks of DMSU riot police quickly cleared the town of innocent bystanders and rioters alike. A total of 25 baton rounds were fired by the police during the day. The number of policemen injured was put at 21 whilst 18 arrests were made.

In the aftermath of the worst rioting Portadown had ever experienced, relations between the police and Unionists sank to an all time low. This resulted in a number of local police officers being evicted from their homes. Complaints were made against the RUC regarding the alleged harassment of local youths. It must be stressed that despite what they had just endured at the hands of the riot police, the Orange Order not only condemned all attacks on policemen's homes but actively campaigned to calm the situation in the town.

It has to be stressed that relationships between the Orange Order and Unionist people in Portadown and the ordinary local RUC personnel remained good. It was recognised that the local Force had little or no influence over events dictated at government and senior RUC level.

Calm Restored

For a few years following 1986 the 12 foot barrier was re-erected at the top of Woodhouse Street to prevent the Sunday church parade and the Twelfth and Thirteenth parades from entering Obins Street. It was an unsightly obstacle which on some occasions stayed in place for over a week much to the annoyance of local shoppers and business men. Token protests were made at the barrier on each occasion as the Portadown Orangemen made it clear that they did not accept the ban on parading part of the Queen's highway.

The situation as it stands now is that on the Sunday parade, the Orangemen make their outward journey to Drumcree via Northway to Corcrain. This route skirts the 'Tunnel' district and still passes in full view of part of Obins Avenue. On the return leg the parade takes the Garvaghy Road route back into town. Protests are still made and there is still a large police presence along the Road, but clashes have been few and the tension seems to have eased.

On the 12 July morning, the country lodges together with the Portadown Ex-Servicemen's LOL 608 and District officers parade along Garvaghy Road. The parade is a dignified one and on the insistence of Orange leaders the bands are forbidden to play party tunes when passing Churchill Park, Ballyoran or Garvaghy Park. The 13 July parades do not now pass through Obins Street.

An uneasy calm has returned to Portadown over the re-routing issue. This, however, is not simply a case of Orangemen accepting the re-routing of its traditional parades, but rather it relates to their desire not to cause havoc or destruction in their own town. Neither do Orangemen want to be in confrontation with the police or army as such confrontation is foreign to such a fraternity which each year declares its allegiance to the Crown.

An Analysis of the Re-routing Problem
Some observations should at this stage be made of the re-routing controversy which will help in appreciating the overall situation. The events that developed in Portadown in the mid-1980s can be seen as a microcosm of the overall situation in the Province. The 1,000 metre stretch of the 'Tunnel', although comprising mostly derelict houses and housing only around 70 families has become a symbol of the so-called struggle. Nationalists and republicans, who viewed themselves as an isolated section of the 'Irish nation' had never endeavoured to

integrate themselves into the Northern Ireland state, although they invariably reaped the rewards of being citizens of the United Kingdom. When the Anglo-Irish Agreement was signed they began to use the new found influence of the Eire government to exert pressure on the British to make Obins Street a no-go area to one of the major elements of Protestantism, namely the Orange Order.

The Orange Order, viewed as the protector of Protestantism, sought to uphold its tradition of walking the Queen's highway in a dignified and disciplined manner, without the slightest intention of causing offence to anyone. The organisation felt betrayed by the British government and offended by the actions of the RUC during the worst periods of trouble in 1985–86. The Orange Order did not openly seek confrontation, with the Security Forces, whilst still standing by its principles.

The British government, prior to the signing of the Anglo-Irish Agreement, had attempted to marginalise the Unionists by taking part in talks with the administration of the Irish Republic. A Prime Minister, doggedly determined to prove she was in control of her party and government, Margaret Thatcher, sought to court the assistance of the Dublin government by proving she had the will to face down any Unionist-Loyalist opposition to her will. As it was, Portadown was isolated, and many Unionists and Orangemen in other parts of the Province did not comprehend what was happening and the implications that could arise.

The Eire government did not recognise Northern Ireland as part of the United Kingdom and sought by the Anglo-Irish Agreement to gain influence into its daily affairs even though it had no political mandate from the people to do so.

The RUC was caught in the vacuum between both sides. Its attempts at 'impartial policing ' brought criticism from all sides not least due to the public image presented by the Chief Constable, Sir John Hermon, who succeeded in alienating his force from all sides.

The ironies of the situation as it now stands, are quite outstanding:
The re-routing of a ten minute Orange

parade away from a 1,000-metre stretch of Obins Street consisting of 70 families to the Garvaghy Road which by-passes three Roman Catholic housing estates, comprising hundreds of homes.

The complaint by Roman Catholic representatives is that they are in virtual siege during the day of the parades. The Orange parade takes less than six minutes to pass along the Garvaghy Road.

The clamour is for the Garvaghy Road parade to be re-routed and that the Orangemen should use the shortest route – the shortest route is through Obins Street!

The accusations are that the Orange parades are triumphalist, coat trailing exercises. If this was the case all of the Orange parades in Portadown would have gone through the 'Tunnel' area, not just a few. The parades in question passed through the 'Tunnel' due to its location as the through road to Drumcree. Only the intransigent dogma in which republicanism is entrenched could view these parades as triumphalist.

The re-routing episode was a gross miscalculation and illustrated a total lack of understanding of tradition and how such actions such as banning parades would affect the local community. What resulted was antagonism between the Unionist people and the police and a continued distrust between Protestants and Roman Catholics. Considerable damage was done to property but this paled into insignificance when the IRA detonated a 2,000-pound bomb in the middle of the town on 22 May 1993.

The whole parades issue had a serious effect on the thinking of Unionists in the town. For perhaps the first time the Unionist population saw they could no longer fully rely on the support of the British Government, whilst at the same time the enemies of the state were aligning themselves closer to the government of the Irish Republic, an alliance that now encompasses Sinn Fein/IRA, the SDLP, Fianna Fail and Fine Gael in the so-called Pan-Nationalist Front. The fruits of this grouping have already come to light in the form of several IRA rallies held in front of the City Hall in Belfast and the re-routing of Orange parades in Belfast, most notably along the Ormeau Road. It remains to be seen which Orange parade is next in line for re-routing, whilst republican parades are allowed to take place unmolested. Republicans are no nearer to recognising the fact that Orange parades are a legitimate expression of the cultural identity of the British people of Northern Ireland. It further makes their demands, for parity of esteem of both traditions, ring hollow.

XI

Portadown District in the 1990s

THE 1990s saw the dawning of a new decade, the last in the twentieth century. The mid-eighties had been a time of uncertainty, and a time in Portadown when many had wondered if Orange parades could return to a carnival atmosphere mixed with the celebrations of the day to provide a spectacle for young and old. As if to dispel the doubters, many of whom had nothing to do with the Order itself, the general public, by their support in coming out to watch the Twelfth demonstrations in the town, and contributing to the normality of the situation helped to remove some of the tension that had enveloped the festivities. The late 1980s did not see the decline in the Orange Order that some of its opponents had prophesied, but in fact what it did achieve was to create a new breed of Orangeman determined that in the future his point of view, and his cultural identity would not be so easily denied.

The Tercentenary Year

The year1990 was the 300th anniversary of the Battle of the Boyne. During that year celebrations took place throughout Ireland to celebrate and commemorate the occasion. A re-enactment of the battle took place in Dungannon Park, trips were arranged to the site of the battle outside Drogheda, exhibitions were held and commemorative stamps were issued by the Eire postal services.

Portadown District held its first Mini-Twelfth parade in the town and this heralded the start of the town's celebrations to mark the event.

The County Twelfth demonstration was held in the south Armagh village of Newtownhamilton. Later in the year, in September, Portadown District joined with brethren from all over the world in Belfast in what was later to be described as one of the largest demonstrations of Orangemen ever held. LOL 608, the Ex-Servicemen's Lodge, had the honour of supplying the Colour Party for County Armagh on that outstanding occasion.

Mini-Twelfth Parades

As mentioned above, the decision was made by the District to hold an annual District parade prior to the Twelfth of July celebration each year. The first such parade was held in 1990 and these became known as the Mini-Twelfth parades. A sub-committee was set up to oversee and organise them and almost immediately they decided that each year the parade should take on a theme to give each year a focus.

The theme for the Mini-Twelfth of 1991 was not hard to find as it was sitting on the doorstep of Portadown District. The year 1991 was the 350th anniversary of the 1641 Rebellion. This 'theme' held particular relevance for the people of Portadown as the River Bann at the town was one of the places where up to two hundred defenceless Protestant men, women, and children were cruelly murdered in 1641. The year of 1991 also marked the 75th anniversary of the Battle of Somme and a wreath-laying ceremony at the town's War Memorial was included in the evening.

The Mini-Twelfth in 1991 took place on 15 June. The District parade, led by St Mark's Silver Band and the Portadown Ex-Servicemen's LOL 608 with the Ulster Special Constabulary LOL 1970 from Sandy Row, Belfast, made their way to the War Memorial where wreaths were laid in memory of the Fallen. The parade now accompanied by a County Tyrone group, The Sword of Gideon Society, representing the rebellion forces, and a group of Portadown Orangemen, Orangewomen and members of the Junior Order, to represent those massacred, made their way to the River Bann where a representation of the 1641 atrocity was staged.

Following the re-enactment a Bible was presented to Bro. Harold Gracey, the Portadown District Master, by a young member of the Junior Order as a symbol of the continued Protestant Faith.

The procession included the Sovereign Grand Master of the Royal Black Institution, Rt. Hon. James Molyneaux MP; the Rev. Martin Smyth MP, Grand Master of the Grand Orange Lodge of Ireland; W. Bro. Norman Hood, Grand Master of the Co. Armagh Grand Orange Lodge; W. Bro. Harold Gracey, District Master Portadown District and representatives of the Women's Loyal Orange Association and the Junior Orange Order. Many visiting brethren accompanied the parade as it made its way out the Lurgan Road and Seagoe Road, past the parish church and churchyard of Seagoe and past the ruins of the old Parish Church before making its way to the Killycomain Road and back through the town centre to Carleton Street Orange Hall. The occasion was given an additional spectacle with the inclusion of a representation of King William's army with a solitary drummer tapping out a slow beat.

Later in the year a commemorative stone, to the memory of those murdered in 1641, was unveiled by the Sovereign Grand Master of the Royal Black Institution, James Molyneaux MP, at a ceremony on the banks of the River Bann. Following the ceremony a lament was played by a piper while Orange brethren scattered rose petals in the water of the river in memory of those who had been so cruelly murdered in October–November 1641.

The following year the Mini-Twelfth parade took as its theme the Ulster-Scots influence on the foundation of America. That year the parade route took in the Brownstown side of the town passing through Edgarstown and the town centre on its return to Carleton Street Orange Hall. These parades were already taking on the character that, as well as having visiting brethren from other Districts they also gave opportunity for the Women's Orange Association and the Junior members to take

part. A further added attraction at each of the parades has been the addition of the Lambeg drums, so much a feature of Orangeism in County Armagh. This was also the first year that an Ulster Society exhibition, 'The Highest Call', which dealt with the Ulster-Scots influence on America, was staged in Carleton Street Orange Hall.

The 1993 Mini-Twelfth took as its theme the influence of Colonel Edward Saunderson MP on the defeat of the Home Rule Bill. The parade took as its route Edenderry and the Killycomain area, passing over the Bann Bridge which Col. Saunderson had used in his speech, so effectively, at the introduction of the second Home Rule Bill of 1893 when he said 'Home Rule may pass this House but it will never pass the Bridge at Portadown'.

The year of 1994 was the 50th anniversary of the D-Day landings. The week prior to the Mini-Twelfth parade an exhibition, again under the auspices of the Ulster Society, was held in Carleton Street Orange Hall and covered the Blitz on Belfast during the Second World War.

On the night of the Mini-Twelfth parade wreaths were laid at the War Memorial in memory of those killed in the conflicts but with special reference to those who lost their lives in the D-Day landings. Bro. Thomas Speers, one of the veterans of the landings, and a Past Master of Johnston's Royal Standard LOL 99, was invited along with the Rev. Martin Smyth, Grand Master of the Grand Lodge of Ireland and W. Bro. Norman Hood, Grand Master of the Co. Armagh Grand Lodge to lay the wreath at the War Memorial. The District parade then made its way along the Armagh Road, Brownstown, Edgarstown and the town centre to Carleton Street Orange Hall.

The year 1994 also saw the establishment of a new Credit Union. Mrs Jennifer McCusker, widow of the late Bro. Harold McCusker, officially opened the new Carleton Credit Unit which has its offices in the former caretaker's house next to the Orange Hall in Carleton Street.

The year 1995 can be described as a special year in all the anniversaries of the Orange Order being the 200th anniversary of its formation. As has been detailed in this book Portadown has played a prominent role in the development of the Order, but its birthplace undoubtedly lies a few miles outside Portadown, at the famous Diamond, near the village of Loughgall.

The year of 1995 belonged to the Diamond and Loughgall District but Portadown like all other districts had its own celebrations. These celebrations were as diverse as they were many, but included an exhibition on the formation of the Orange Order, again in conjunction with the Ulster Society. In order to allow a greater number of people to visit the exhibition it was held in the Town Hall, Portadown. The exhibition took place during the week preceding the now annual pre-Twelfth District parade of 10 June. The parade made its way through the town to the cemetery at Seagoe where a wreath was laid at the grave of the Blacker family, the family from Portadown so instrumental in establishing the Orange Order in the area and beyond.

The inclusion and the diversity of the events enabled many people, from both inside and outside the Orange Order, to learn more about the Order and its origins and to develop a closer understanding of Orange principles.

Anniversary Church Parades

The Twelfth demonstrations and Boyne Anniversary Church parades have continued throughout the 1990s.

Perhaps the most contentious of the parades, the annual church service at Drumcree, has continued to take place. The Drumcree church parade of 1995 was to achieve particular prominence as detailed in Chapter XII.

All too often, in the past, the other District church parades that take place in Portadown and the surrounding area have received little attention except for adequate coverage in the local press. This is quite naturally because they do not carry with them the same quality of sensationalism as those parades deemed by others as controversial and do not win political points or argument. It would be wrong, however, to neglect mentioning them on these pages.

Each year church parades are held to the different denominational Protestant churches in Portadown. The annual July Anniversary parades take place to Drumcree Parish Church, already mentioned, Mullavilly Parish Church, with brethren from Tandragee District, and Seagoe Parish Church with brethren from Lurgan District. There also takes place a parade and service to St Saviour's at the Dobbin on the Armagh side of Portadown. At the end of October, each year, a further church parade and service takes place on Reformation Sunday. This service is rotated around the various churches in the town. The Orange Order is an organisation that draws its membership from all of the Reformed Protestant churches and as such enjoys the fellowship with these churches during parades and services. All too often there are those opposed to the Orange Order who are quick to advance the case of the Orange Order being *sectarian*, however, the Orange Order, while it serves as an umbrella organisation for Protestantism, can only be deemed sectarian by those who would corrupt the true meaning of the word.

Twelfth Demonstrations

The County Twelfth demonstrations of 1991 and 1992 were held in Markethill and Bessbrook respectively. The Portadown brethren joined with their County brethren at these parades after firstly parading through Portadown. Each year, since the war years, it has become the custom in the Portadown District parade in the town, that in the morning a wreath is laid at the War Memorial in memory of the Fallen. This ceremony is carried out by the District officers with the able assistance of the Ex-Servicemen's LOL 608 who form the guard of honour. The dignity and solemnity of this ceremony has become so highly regarded that an increasing number of visitors from outside the Portadown area make a point of coming to Portadown in the morning to witness the ceremony before making their way to other demonstration sites. In 1991 it was suggested by the District Master Harold Gracey, and accepted by District lodge, that each year the Worshipful Masters of each of the lodges in the District should accompany the District officers at the head of the parade leaving Carleton Street and be present at the ceremony at the War Memorial. Following the ceremony the Masters return to join their own lodges for the rest of the parade. This has now become a feature of the Twelfth District parade.

The year 1993 saw the County demonstration return to Portadown. In the early 1960s the policy had been adopted by the County Grand Lodge that the venues for the annual County demonstration should be strictly determined by the order of the District numbers. This afforded each District to be aware, well in advance, of when they would have to host the County demonstration. However, before it was to become the turn of Portadown District to host the demonstration in 1993, no amount of prior notice could have prepared them for events that would occur in the town in the Spring of that year.

The 22 May 1993 was an ordinary Saturday for most people in Portadown. Shoppers were making their way about town oblivious to an event that was unfolding directly before their eyes. IRA terrorists were in the process of placing a 2,000lb bomb in the town centre, the result of which would be to cause maximum damage with no concern for life or limb of anyone in town that day. The van containing the device was left in front of the Halifax Building Society, near the entrance to Woodhouse Street. No warning was given and it was only because of the splendid efforts of police on the ground and the co-operation of the general public in clearing the area, that carnage was averted. In the resultant explosion the town centre was devastated, like a number of others which had received the same treatment from the IRA. Again Portadown was to be flashed across the television screens and newspapers of the world. Long after the media had ceased to show interest shop and business owners would still be involved in the work of trying to get their premises up and running, whilst those who had received injuries would continue to need treatment for many months and those who had been in town that day and escaped any injury would reflect on what might have been. This event was seen not only as an assault on the commercial heart of the town but was also viewed as an assault on the heart of Orangeism only a few months before the

County demonstration was to be held in the town.

The 1993 County Twelfth demonstration took place in Portadown as planned. The evening before the demonstration, the Eleventh Night, bonfires were ablaze at Brownstown, Edgarstown, Killycomain and Mournview Street. From early the next morning the town was alive to the sound of bands, as the brethren of the District made their way to Carleton Street Orange Hall, ablaze with colour from flags, bunting, arches and of course, Orange regalia. That year, as the brethren of the County made their way through the shell of the town centre, a town centre that for days and nights had been alive to the sounds of contractors working on the damaged buildings, there was an increased strength in the resolve of all brethren that those who had perpetrated such damage should be resisted to the fullest degree.

The demonstration made its way to the field at the Loughgall Road from Edenderry, crossing the Bann Bridge, headed by the County Grand Master, W. Bro. Norman Hood, and the County officers as well as Portadown District Master W. Bro. Harold Gracey and his District officers. The day was a success for the brethren of Portadown District despite all that had gone before and although at times the parade looked as though it was taking place in war-torn Bosnia the overall spectacle and festival of the day was maintained and enjoyed by the many thousands of visitors to the town. Later in the year a special dinner was held in Carleton Street Orange Hall by way of a 'thank you' to those brethren who had been involved with the local organisation of the day.

The County demonstration of 1994 was held in the village of Richhill, a rather inclement day that, although curtailing the Lambeg drummers, none-the-less did not dampen the enthusiasm of the brethren or spectators on the day.

The dawning of 1995 was the start of a special year for the County of the Diamond. This was to be the year when the eyes of all Orange brethren throughout the world would be on the County Armagh village of Loughgall.

It was regrettable that the County Grand

Master W. Bro. Norman Hood, who during 1994 had worked so hard to set in place the County Armagh arrangements for the Bi-centenary celebrations, and who was held in very high esteem by all brethren, died during a trip to New Zealand, where he was attending the 38th meeting of the Imperial Orange Council of the World.

Many Districts had arranged their own Bi-centenary celebrations and events and an outdoor event incorporating a pageant and fireworks display was staged at Windsor Park, Belfast. As it turned out, the Armagh County Twelfth demonstration was scheduled for Loughgall in 1995, and this enabled a rehearsal for the forthcoming major Bi-centennial demonstration in September.

The Bi-centenary of the Orange Order
The 200th anniversary of the Battle of the Diamond and the formation of the Orange Order had as its main focus the Armagh village of Loughgall. On 21 September Portadown brethren assembled with brethren of the County at the Diamond Orange Hall. They paraded to the site of the famous battle where a monument was unveiled to commemorate the battle and the founding of the Orange Order.

The following Saturday, 23 September 1995, there took place in Loughgall village a huge demonstration comprising Orange brethren from throughout the world. The different counties formed up at various assembly points before making their way into the village. Armagh County formed up at the Diamond Orange Hall and headed by Loughgall District paraded to the village. This parade was different in content to most other demonstrations as all lodges did not carry individual banners and paraded together in District order, five abreast, in their Counties with only County and District bannerettes at their head. The only lodge banners permitted on parade, due to their association with the formation of the Order were: LOL 2 Lieutenant Sinclair's Rising Sons, Derryscollop; LOL 85 The Diamond Memorial; and LOL 118 Diamond Grange, all from Loughgall District. Armagh County was headed by the County Grand Master W. Bro. Norman Allen, and led by a massed silver band made up of various bands from the County.

The demonstration was organised in this fashion because had each lodge formed itself on parade in its usual form, with its own band and banner, such a huge contingent of brethren would have taken not hours, but days to pass a given point. This event was recorded as one of the largest gatherings of Orangemen ever seen anywhere in the world.

Due to their stand for 'Civil and Religious Liberty' at the Siege of Drumcree the hundreds of brethren from Portadown, including many members recently initiated at a special District meeting, received a hero's welcome as they paraded through Loughgall. Events at Drumcree were to prove that 200 years later the Orange Institution is as important as ever.

XII

The Siege of Drumcree

EVEN as this history of Orangeism in Portadown District was being written, momentous events were beginning to unfold in the Province. Two events stand out at this moment: one was the paramilitary 'ceasefires' with the accompanying suggestions for political change, whilst the other was the *Siege of Drumcree*, an event which would reaffirm, if that was necessary, Portadown's place as the 'Orange Citadel'.

The Ceasefires

No one could have foreseen that after a campaign of murder, violence and intimidation lasting twenty-five years and leaving over three thousand people dead that the Provisional IRA would call a halt to their terrorist activities. On 31 August 1994 the republican terror group announced a cessation of violence. A few weeks later, in response, the Combined Loyalist Military Command representing the UVF and UFF followed suit and announced their own ceasefire.

Many people, on both sides, were sceptical as to the sincerity of the ceasefire announcements, scepticism which has remained unabated given the continuation of punishment beatings and racketeering. The return to street politics and agitation, particularly by Sinn Féin, together with the refusal of the IRA to surrender arms, ammunition and explosives has fuelled the speculation that the IRA ceasefire is a temporary change of tactics.

Pressure from the so called Pan Nationalist Front consisting of the SDLP, Sinn Féin, Fine Gael and Fianna Fail, together with the support of US President Bill Clinton resulted in the joint publication of the Framework Document, a document heavily in favour of Irish nationalism. Convicted republican terrorists have been released from jails in the Irish republic whilst growing pressure has been brought to bear on the British government to release terrorists from Northern Ireland prisons.

Republicans have been given concession after concession whilst the democratically expressed wishes of the Unionist population have been ignored. The banning of the National Anthem at Queen's University has been followed by increased agitation against the dignified and traditional parades of the Orange Order. The campaign to re-route Orange parades is, as Portadown brethren know, nothing new, however, the agitation was to increase dramatically in the ceasefire period.

Parade Re-routing

Easter 1995 was to see the re-routing of parades issue once again brought to the fore. In Belfast the Lower Ormeau Concerned Community stepped up its campaign to have Orange loyalist parades re-routed away from their area. They met with success. Parades were re-routed in 'the interests of public order' according to the police, when counter demonstrations were held by the Lower Ormeau Community group.

As time went on it was becoming increasingly inevitable that the re-routing issue in Portadown would be brought to prominence again exactly a decade after the earlier parades controversy in the town.

Contact had been established between the Lower Ormeau Concerned Community, buoyed by their recent success, and a group of Garvaghy Road residents who were also determined to have Orange parades stopped from passing along their traditional route. The *Portadown Times* of 26 May reported that following a meeting at the Drumcree Community Centre a committee had been set up of Garvaghy residents:

> to express the opposition of the vast majority of the residents in this predominately Catholic/Nationalist area to the continued routing of Orange marches through the area

The group asked for a meeting with the RUC and also sent a letter to the Orange Order requesting a meeting.

On 9 June under the banner headline 'Call for talks on marches' the *Portadown Times* reported that the Garvaghy Road Residents Group had made contact with the Secretary of State, Sir Patrick Mayhew, concerning the parades issue. They had also had a meeting with the RUC. This meeting was described as 'totally unsatisfactory' as the police had quoted the Public Order Order as the only grounds they would have to re-route the parade. This, they said, could only be invoked if there was threat to public order with major disruption. No reply had been received by the Garvaghy group from the Orange Order.

The Debate Continues

The debate via the local media continued, In the *Portadown Times* of 23 June sources from within the Orange Order were noted as saying that the Order was not prepared to become embroiled in a debate with individuals whom they considered did not represent the people of the Garvaghy area. It was felt that it was due to the successes at the lower Ormeau to re-route parades that attention was now being turned to Portadown. It was pointed out in the report that while the Orange Order had previously paraded:

six or seven times through Obins Street over the July period, plus the return march on Drumcree Sunday. This is down to two and the Garvaghy group still isn't satisfied with the compromise.

Two other groups entered the debate, The Mid Ulster Brigade of the UVF said in a statement referring to the Garvaghy residents:

It is ironic that a section of our people who call for parity of esteem and equality are the very people who refuse the same rights to their fellow British citizens.

Two Craigavon Alliance councillors urged the Orange Order to issue a statement accepting that Civil and Religious Liberty should include the rights of all legitimate organisations to parade in town centres on appropriate occasions. The Alliance statement failed however to clarify its meaning of 'a legitimate' organisation or 'appropriate occasions'.

The Upper Garvaghy residents in their statement reported in the *Portadown Times* of 30 June stated their intention to hold:

peaceful public protest on Sunday July 9 and on the morning of the Twelfth to coincide with the Orange marches through the area.

A spokesman for the group was reported as saying:

the people of Garvaghy simply don't want the Orange parades coming through

Such a statement hinted little at the spirit of 'compromise'.

Other Factors

Within a few days a development had occurred that would cause widespread civil unrest and have an effect on attitudes.

At 6.30 a.m. on Monday 3 July Private Lee Clegg, a member of the Parachute Regiment was released from Wakefield Prison. He had spent four years in custody for the murder of joyrider Karen Reilly in West Belfast on 30 September 1990. Clegg was released on licence signed by the Secretary of State Sir Patrick Mayhew.

Over the following two days there was serious rioting in nationalist areas which resulted in eight million pounds worth of damage being caused. Feelings were running high at the time due to the release of prisoners issue. The RUC were quoted as saying that on the Monday 240 petrol bombs were thrown with 470 on Tuesday. There were 160 highjackings on Monday and 12 on Tuesday. 'Several' people were arrested.

For the Orangemen in Portadown it again appeared that during scenes of extreme street violence led by republicans and nationalists the police were reluctant to take meaningful action. However, the *News Letter* reported on 5 July:

Upwards of 1000 police will be on duty in

Portadown on Sunday during the Orange Orders pre-Twelfth church parade to Drumcree.

On the evening of 5 July a mini-Twelfth Orange parade was again prevented from parading over the Ormeau Bridge by police. To avoid confrontation with nationalists, members of Ballynafeigh District Lodge had taken the decision to walk a circuit leading them up Annadale Embankment. Trouble erupted later when some loyalist demonstrators attempted to pass through police lines.

A parade package for the forthcoming Twelfth was offered by the Lower Ormeau Concerned Community to the Orangemen. This 'allowed' the Orange brethren to walk through the nationalist enclave of the Ormeau on the Twelfth on condition no other parades would pass that way until the end of 1996. This package was labelled as blackmail by the Ballynafeigh District Secretary

In Bellaghy, Co. Londonderry, republican protesters were prevented by police from halting a traditional loyalist band parade through the main street of the village.

The Portadown situation was yet to come. Against this backdrop and in the interests of keeping the situation calm the Portadown District Lodge had not allowed themselves to become involved in public debate but on 7 July they published a statement outlining their position. This statement is reproduced in full.

Challenge for Peace and Calm at Annual Church Parade to Drumcree

For almost 200 years the Orangemen of Portadown have paraded with dignity to and from the mother church at Drumcree causing no offence. As a religious organisation we believe in civil and religious liberty. The anniversary church parade to Drumcree Parish Church is the oldest recorded Orange Service in the history of the Orange Institution. In the inaugural year the Reverend Stewart Blacker (Rector of Drumcree) also a prominent Orangeman of Portadown preached the sermon to the Orangemen of Portadown. Successive generations of Portadown Orangemen have at-

tended Divine Service in Drumcree Parish Church on an annual basis and the Rector of the parish has conducted the service on all occasions.

The parade route the most direct and only one available at that time was traditionally through Obins Street on the outward leg of the journey, the return journey being via the Garvaghy Road passing close to recently constructed housing estates that originally had a mixed population. It is only during the period of the recent "Troubles" and the subsequent demographic changes in the Obins Street/Garvaghy Road area that there has been some opposition to these annual Orange parades. Always conscious of the feelings of the local residents of the Garvaghy Road, the Orange Institution has been at pains to avoid confrontation and to conduct themselves with the utmost decorum as befitting a religious organisation parading to and from divine worship. Indeed impartial observers have commented favourably on this conduct.

Over the years and especially since the rerouting episode in 1985–86 Portadown Orangemen have shown themselves to be able to parade with dignity over the parades issue, whilst still maintaining its preference for the traditional route. May we also point out that the Garvaghy Road is the main thoroughfare linking the Dungannon – Moy and motorway roads with Portadown town centre. The then Chief Constable Sir John Hermon personally inspected and approved this route on that basis.

It is regrettable that a minority of residents of the housing estates located on either side of this thoroughfare have chosen to create divisions between themselves and their fellow townspeople, we feel sure that this aggressive confrontational approach is not welcomed by most people residing in the Garvaghy Road area. Orange Order parades in the Obins Street/Garvaghy Road area have a history and tradition dating back to the time when nationalists raised no objection to these parades. Discipline and determination not to give offence despite extreme provocation has been a feature of the Orange parades to and from Drumcree with no breach by those on parade ever having been committed.

As an addition to this it was recorded in the *News Letter* of 7 July that rather than being intransigent, as they were often accused by opponents, the Portadown Orange brethren had adhered to five 'compromises' over the preceding ten years:

1. Only two Orange parades passed along the Garvaghy Road – One on the return from Drumcree Parish Church and the other on the morning of the 12 July.
2. No Orange or Royal Black parades now pass through Obins Street.
3. Only a limited number of bands take part in the two parades along Garvaghy Road.
4. Bands are permitted only to play hymns or suitable march music.
5. Bands do not play when passing the Roman Catholic Chapel.

On Thursday 6 July police removed twenty Irish tricolours which had been flying along the upper Garvaghy Road for a number of months. The local Residents Association called this action 'an act of provocation by a police force that is the backbone of the Orange Order'. (The *Portadown Times* 7/7/95.)

The Pre-parade Situation

The position as the weekend of the Drumcree parade approached was then as follows. During a period of ten months the Unionist population, while giving thanks for the ceasefire, had watched as concession after concession had been given by the British government to those of the Pan-Nationalist Front.

Due to the situation on the streets, punishment beatings and petrol bombings, the ceasefire was viewed by many as a 'phoney peace.'

Legal Orange Order, and other loyalist parades had been re-routed by police in the interests of public order due to illegal street demonstrations by a section of the community traditionally opposed to all that these loyal orders stood for.

Portadown District Lodge had given the statutory notice to the local police stating its intention to parade the 'traditional' route to Drumcree, outward via Obins Street, inward via Garvaghy Road to Carleton Street

Orange Hall. On Saturday 8 July the Portadown District Lodge secretary was informed by the local police that the outward journey would have to be via Northway and not Obins Street. No indication was given at that time of any problem surrounding the Garvaghy Road return route.

The Garvaghy Road residents group had stated their intention of holding a protest against the Orange parade on the Sunday. They also gave notice of their intention to parade from the Garvaghy Road through the town centre to Carleton Street Orange Hall at 10 a.m. to coincide with the start of the Orange parade. During their press conference the previous Tuesday, attended by their officials, Gerald Kelly, Donald Mercer and Eamon Stack (Jesuit Priest) it was stated:

> We're determined to put a stop to this yearly triumphalism, through our area.

The Roman Catholic Primate of all Ireland Cardinal Cathal Daly sent a letter of support to the Garvaghy Residents Association in support of their peaceful protest.

The RUC were said to be drafting into the Portadown area a force of over one thousand police officers. This was all occurring against a back drop of republican street violence as a result of the Lee Clegg release.

Darkness fell on Saturday 8 July on Portadown, a town of rising tension.

Sunday 9 July

The morning of Sunday 9 July arrived in glorious sunshine. Orange brethren had begun assembling in Carleton Street from as early as 9 a.m.

At 9.45 a.m. the Garvaghy Residents' Association with a reported three hundred marchers, attempted to make their way into the town centre *en route* to Carleton Street. The parade was stopped at Woodside Green by the police. An earlier offer by the police for the group to parade to Carleton Street between 6.00 a.m. and 8.30 a.m. had been rejected by the marchers.

At the police line Brendan McKenna[1], leader of the Garvaghy group, read out a letter he had hoped to deliver to Carleton Street Orange Hall to the assembled crowd and added that he hoped the same public order legislation would be used by the police to block the Orange marchers.

Just before 10.30 a.m. Portadown District Lodge led by District Master Bro. Harold Gracey, the District officers, Bro. David Trimble MP and the Ex-Servicemen's LOL 608 Colour Party started their walk to Drumcree. Accompanied by two bands, Edgarstown Accordion and the Star of David Accordion, the eight hundred brethren paraded through the town centre, along Northway, past Corcrain and on to Drumcree Parish Church. Along the route crowds of spectators, the largest in years, watched the procession in the warm morning sunshine.

On arrival at Drumcree Parish Church the Orangemen filed into the church and packed the adjoining church hall to join in the 11.30 service conducted by the Rector of Drumcree, the Rev. John Pickering.

The Siege Begins

Following the service the Orangemen left the church. As they did so they were confronted with a fleet of grey police Land Rovers positioned on the road at the bottom of Drumcree Hill. Having been first given the indication that the Land Rovers were there to offer protection to the Orangemen *en route* along the Garvaghy Road the police quickly revised their statement informing the District officers that the parade would not be allowed to proceed along its traditional route. However, the legality of this decision seemed uncertain as no such order or notice was served by the police.

At this stage the District Master, accompanied by Bro. David Trimble, spoke with the senior police officers. At first the police were vague in their response to questions raised by Bros. Gracey and Trimble in relation to the clearing of the Garvaghy Road by their officers. On confirmation of this the District Master spoke to the assembled brethren. He explained the situation and told them he had clearly informed the police:

The brethren of Portadown will not be moving let it be hours, let it be days, let it be weeks. We are for staying until such times as we can walk our traditional route, down the Garvaghy Road.

This statement was greeted by loud cheers of approval from the assembled Orangemen. With three grey Land Rovers positioned across the road, separating the police from the Orangemen, a standoff position had been reached.

At the same time as these events were taking place the Garvaghy protesters were staging a sit down protest at the junction of the Ashgrove Road. Although the police informed the five hundred strong crowd that they were breaking the law they made no attempt to remove them. This protest lasted into the afternoon when the protesters dispersed following reassurances from the RUC that the Orange Parade would not be allowed along the Garvaghy Road.

The standoff position now became the focus of media attention. The District Master, Bro. Harold Gracey and Member of Parliament Bro. David Trimble were about to begin a period of negotiation that was to last for almost forty-eight hours.

The Orangemen Consolidate Their Position

As time passed it became clear that the police had underestimated the resolve of the Orangemen to remain at Drumcree. Within an hour of the standoff beginning provisions began to arrive at the church hall and under the management of a team of ladies a 'field kitchen' was soon in operation. During the following days many items of food stuffs arrived not only from the surrounding local areas but from as far afield as Ballynahinch and Comber. A seemingly tireless band of ladies continued to provide refreshments for the Orangemen both by day and during the long hours of the night.

Tension remained high during the day. Groups of Orange brethren took it in turn to stand in vigil at the police lines. Television and radio news bulletins described the scene at Drumcree. Bro. Harold Gracey made an appeal during an early interview for all available Orange brethren to come to Drumcree. This request was broadcast by only one radio station amidst allegations that the RUC had exercised censorship. Any attempted censorship failed however due to the numerous mobile communication devices in the possession of Orange brethren.

Telephone calls were made directly to County and District officers throughout the Province. The police also attempted to play down the number of Orange brethren staying in Drumcree. Their count of two hundred Orangemen was conservative to say the least.

During the afternoon, as word filtered through to the town of the Drumcree standoff, residents began blocking roads to Corcrain and at the Shillington Bridge. They stated their intention to remain at the blockades until the Orangemen returned home via Garvaghy Road.

At Drumcree small groups of Orangemen periodically made their way across fields towards the back of the police lines. These forays were designed to test the police reactions. During one of these clashes, at the Land Rovers, an Orangeman and two policemen received slight injuries.

It was soon clearly evident that while the police riot gear afforded the wearers protection during riot situations in urban areas it became more of a hindrance in open fields and whilst clambering over hedges. It was also clear that strategically the Orangemen were at an advantage being able to look down on and behind the police lines from their vantage point atop Drumcree Hill.

As the evening drew on it became obvious that the Portadown District Lodge would not be able to attend the annual evening church service at Seagoe Parish Church. The brethren therefore formed up at Drumcree Church Hall, shortly after 8.30 p.m. and paraded down to the police lines, where a short service was held conducted by Wor. Bro. the Rev. Percy Patterson, County Grand Chaplain, and the Rev. John Pickering.

Arrangements were now being formulated to hold a mass rally on the Monday evening at Drumcree. As brethren from throughout Northern Ireland began arriving on the Sunday evening they were told of this development. Some stayed and settled in for the night while others left to make arrangements for the following day.

Portadown District's stand for Civil and Religious Liberty received the backing of the County Armagh Grand Orange Lodge. Calls were made to hold the County Twelfth

demonstration at Drumcree if the standoff continued over the Twelfth period.

Other Protests Mounted

Orangemen mounted protests at several other locations in support of the Portadown brethren. Protests were held in Belfast, outside Willowfield RUC Station and at Donegall Pass Police Station. Roads were blocked in the South Derry village of Tobermore and around one hundred Orangemen held a protest in Ahoghill, Co. Antrim.

At 10.30 p.m. a cheer went up from the crowd at the appearance of the DUP leader, the Rev. Ian Paisley, as he made his way down Drumcree Hill towards the Land Rovers. After spending some time in conversation with Bro. Harold Gracey and Bro. David Trimble he spoke with senior police officers. Before leaving for Belfast to meet the Deputy Chief Constable Blair Wallace, Dr Paisley spoke to the assembled crowd adding his support to their struggle and advising them to exercise restraint even under the greatest provocation. Later, in the early hours of Monday morning, the Rev. Ian Paisley returned from Belfast. His meeting with the Deputy Chief Constable had proved unsuccessful.

Armed with this news the Orange brethren prepared themselves for the long vigil throughout the night but support for their plight was growing, growing at a greater rate than anyone that evening could have foreseen.

Drumcree Siege – Day 2

Awakening on the Monday morning, from where they had spent the night in the church hall, in tents and even in the open, the Orange brethren were heartened to learn of the support being given to their stand throughout the country. As one Orangeman put it, 'It is not so much what we do here that counts but what others do at other places that will see this to its conclusion.' Drumcree had become the symbol of Protestant/Unionist frustration.

Food continued to arrive. Any fears that the momentum of support was beginning to wane were scorched as the time of the evening rally approached. Throughout the day the vigil was maintained at the police road block. Bands and Lambeg drummers marched down to the police lines and the crowds kept growing. From six o'clock in the evening they began arriving in earnest. They arrived in cars from all parts of the Province, parking as close as they could to Drumcree, then continuing on foot.

The Massed Rally

The rally, held in a large field behind Drumcree church, had been planned to start at 7.00 p.m. However, it was delayed for over an hour to facilitate the arrival of those caught up in traffic. During the delay the crowds were entertained by bands and the sound of the Lambegs. Estimates of the size of the crowd varied between 25,000 and 50,000, however, there was no disputing the fact that this was one of the largest gatherings of Orangemen ever seen in the Portadown area.

The rally eventually commenced under the chairmanship of Wor. Bro. Norman Allen, County Grand Master. Speeches were made by the Portadown District Master, Bro. Harold Gracey; Bro. David Trimble MP; Wor. Bro. Jeffrey Donaldson, Assistant Grand Master; the Rev. Ian Paisley and Wor. Bro. Bain, the Grand Master of Scotland, who offered the fullest support of the Scottish Brethren. As the platform speeches continued some violence flared at the police lines but contrary to press reports this violence was not as a result of a speech delivered by the Rev. Ian Paisley. Media reports had given the impression that it was after his speech and because of it that the flare-up started. The trouble started before the Rev. Ian Paisley had in fact addressed the gathering. Dr John Alderdice, leader of the Alliance Party, made a determined effort to make political capital out of this piece of misinformation.

The trouble involved the throwing of some missiles at the police. The police replied with plastic baton rounds. Following the rally the Orangemen accompanied by bands paraded down to the police roadblock. After some jostling, the Rev. Ian Paisley, Ian Paisley Jun., Bros. Harold Gracey, David Trimble and members of Comber District Lodge succeeded in making their way through the police lines in order to speak to senior police officers. Some trouble continued between police and the crowd with more plastic baton rounds being fired. The crowd were able to outflank the police and on a number of occasions managed to cut off riot squad officers from their colleagues. A number of police officers and Orangemen were injured but in relation to the size of the assembled crowd injuries were minimal. The situation eventually settled around 10.30 p.m. the crowd reassured by the news that negotiations were in progress. The level of violence had much less intensity and fell far short of that which was reported by the media the following day.

Negotiations and First Indications of a Parade

In the meantime the Portadown District Master, Bro. Harold Gracey, Bro. David Trimble MP and Rev. Ian Paisley were transported by the police to Edward Street RUC Station where negotiations resumed. At around 10.30 Bro. David Trimble was summoned to listen to Brendan McAllister (and thereby waste a lot of time) at the Church hall. While there both he and Bro. Jeffrey Donaldson were re-called to the police station at around 11.00 p.m. to continue the negotiations. Just before 1.00 a.m. an agreement, which would allow Portadown District to parade along the Garvaghy Road, was reached.

Back at the road block at Drumcree the members of Portadown District Lodge waited. Orangemen from other Districts either made their way into Portadown to await the arrival of the Portadown brethren or waited at Drumcree. Distrust of the police remained high with many believing this was simply a ploy by them to get as many visiting brethren to leave the area as possible.

News of the impending march spread quickly and in Portadown crowds gathered at Shillington Bridge in anticipation of the parades arrival. These numbers swelled and a band paraded the town as the gathering crowds waited.

The Orange negotiators returned to Drumcree to inform the assembled brethren that an agreement had finally been hammered out. Portadown brethren began to assemble at the Church hall for the expected parade to begin. Meanwhile the press had carried reports of the deal to the Garvaghy Road where between 1.30 and 2.00 a.m. residents were forced from their homes to block the road. This action resulted in the police losing their nerve once more.

As the Orangemen waited they were told by police of this street protest. They were informed that the parade would be allowed through when the protest had been cleared. Information received by the Orangemen via their own sources told them the police were making no attempt to clear the road. As the time went on the Orangemen became resolved to the fact that no parade would happen that night. Between 5.30 a.m. and 6.00 a.m. the Orange negotiating team gave the police the ultimatum that unless the situation was resolved by 8.00 a.m. Tuesday all negotiations would cease. Plans began to be made to escalate the level of protests throughout the surrounding area and the Province should this occur.

Throughout the night protests had been taking place in many areas. The port of Larne was blocked by Orangemen as was, amongst other places, Shaftsbury Square in Belfast and towns in County Antrim.

The Parade Gets the Go Ahead

It was shortly after 9.00 a.m. that Portadown District Lodge members were informed that the parade would go ahead along its traditional route of the Garvaghy Road. The one condition attached was that only Portadown District members would be allowed to parade.

The brethren were requested to move back up Drumcree Hill away from the police road block to allow them to remove the Land Rovers. This was done.

Shortly after 10.30 a.m. Portadown District Lodge formed up on Drumcree Hill behind their District Standard. Following the removal of the police road block and under the instruction of their Worshipful District Master the parade moved off on its return journey to Carleton Street Orange Hall, to the applause of the visiting brethren.

On a damp grey morning the only sound to break the silence was the noise of eight hundred marching feet as the Orangemen of Portadown District started along the

Drumcree Road on the return route to Portadown, forty-six hours late. The parade turned left onto the Garvaghy Road where a crowd of less than one hundred nationalist protesters stood across the road at the old Mayfair factory. As the brethren approached, the protesters moved to the footpaths and stood in silence as the parade passed by. No words or comments were exchanged. To the sound of marching feet the Orangemen passed the silent protesters, up past Woodside Hill along Parkmount towards the town. As the parade rounded the right hand bend at the carpet factory entrance and came within sight of those waiting at the Shillington Bridge a cheer went up.

At Park Road corner there were remarkable scenes with the waiting crowds cheering and waving flags. The cheering continued as the parade, now joined by bands, visiting brethren, Bro. David Trimble and the Rev. Ian Paisley proceeded through the town centre to Carleton Street Orange Hall. The town was at a stand still as cheering shoppers, workers and friends welcomed the Orange brethren home. No police presence was evident in the town centre, the police having been recalled to barracks.

On arrival at Carleton Street the Orange brethren applauded the Portadown District Master as he made his way down the Orange ranks. Bro. David Trimble and the Rev. Ian Paisley, with linked hands, also walked along the ranks to cheers and applause.

Following these scenes the road blocks were removed from roads throughout the Province. Other planned demonstrations, protests and actions formulated should the parade not have gone through were stood down.

The Drumcree Sunday Orange parade that should have taken a maximum of fifteen minutes to pass through Garvaghy Road was finally over after an unprecedented forty-eight hour delay.

Post Script

Immediately following the return of the Orangemen the RUC PR machine began a face saving exercise on behalf of the police. The operation to re-route the parade had been ill-conceived and had underestimated the resilience of the Orange brethren to see to the end the standoff. Drumcree had become more of an issue than the simple routing of an Orange Parade. It provided the platform for a United Loyalist front, a section of the population frustrated at being taken for granted and ignored for so long.

Newspapers carried reports that the RUC had been divided over the handling of the Drumcree situation. The *Belfast Telegraph* of 11 July reported:

> relationships between various police figures had become so strained that at one point yesterday the Chief Constable, Sir Hugh Annesley, was almost asked by a senior officer to intervene in order to guarantee a clear decisive command on the ground.

Orangemen present at Drumcree had witnessed at first hand the clear divisions within the police. This was further borne out at the end of the standoff when two senior police officers from Belfast had come to Portadown to oversee the parade along the Garvaghy Road.

Much publicity was given to the part played by Brendan McAllister of the Northern Ireland Mediation Network during the 'negotiations'. While Mr McAllister may have had input with the police and the Garvaghy residents he had no part to play in negotiations with those representing the Portadown Orange District.

It was also reported that part of the so-called deal involved re-routing the Twelfth of July Orange parade of the country lodges that made their way along the Garvaghy Road early in the morning *en route* to Carleton Street. As detailed in an earlier chapter this was a compromise reached a decade earlier with the police following the re-routing of Orange parades from Obins Street. As usual on the Twelfth morning the country lodges were turned away from the traditional Obins Street route by the police. A letter of protest was given to the police by the District Master. The lodges then took an alternative route to Carleton Street Orange Hall.

On the Twelfth of July morning the Ballynafeigh District Lodge brethren were successful in parading along the lower Ormeau Road despite orchestrated protests.

So ended what has since become known as the *Siege of Drumcree*. This episode will surely go down in history alongside the other famous stands for Civil and Religious Liberty made by the loyalist people of Ulster. The Portadown Orange brethren, with the support of brethren and friends from throughout the Province, had shown what could be achieved by people power in what was largely a peaceful standoff.

Regrettably there have been those whose only wish is to exploit the situation for their own ends. Following the end of the Drumcree episode a sectarian program of attacks on Orange halls and Protestant church halls commenced. The Drumcree Church Hall had a petrol bomb hurled at its front door, fortunately, unlike many other halls, it caused little damage. One wonders what the future holds and what type of future political structures can accommodate all sides. On the evidence seen to date it seems the spirit of compromise from the nationalist/republican standpoint actually means domination over those with whom they do not agree.

The Orange Order has now been in existence for two hundred years and has continued to exist through times when its enemies sought to destroy it. Perhaps those men all those years ago, who fought at the Battle of the Diamond and founded the Institution, never considered that their organisation would still be around as we approach the year 2000 and the beginning of the third millennium. They could hardly have foreseen that today, as in 1795, the cultural identity, heritage and faith of the Ulster Protestant would still be under threat and that the Orange Institution would still be needed to defend civil and religious liberty two hundred years later. The cause of each individual member of the Orange Institution is as important and as great today as it has ever been in the safeguarding of the principles of the Order. Today, we are the custodians of these principles. We hold them in trust. They are the legacy of future generations.

XIII

Profiles of District Masters of the Twentieth Century

William John Locke JP (DM 1891–1905)

A tall, powerfully built man, sporting a bushy beard common to the period, W. J. Locke was every inch an imposing and significant figure. He held the office of District Master during the uncertain events beginning to unfold at the turn of the century. His death in 1905 was a serious blow to the Orange Institution in Portadown, but Bro. Locke's influence on the development of the Orange Order in the area has not been forgotten.

William John Locke was instrumental in the planning and provision of an Orange hall that would serve the needs of the Order in what was (and still is) regarded as the 'Orange Citadel'. It was through his dedication that work began on the hall in 1873 and was completed in 1875. Never one to rest on his laurels Bro. Locke soon made more plans to expand the accommodation of Carleton Street Orange Hall and at his instigation a reading room, library and recreational facilities were added in 1882.

Although the head of the family's coach making business, and therefore extremely busy in overseeing the firm, W. J. Locke was a tireless worker for the cause of Orangeism. He was Master of his own private lodge, LOL 40, in addition to being the Master of Portadown District LOL 1. Whilst in office Locke ruled the District with a rod of iron, laying down a strict code of discipline which he expected everyone to adhere to. As the Master of Portadown Orangemen W. J. Locke always took time to make frequent visits to the many lodges within Portadown District and his presence at any private lodge meeting was always an event eagerly anticipated.

One interesting item in the District minutes refers to a resolution which was passed in 1892, just one year after the election of Bro. Locke to the Master's chair. The resolution stated that 'no carriages, vehicles or brakes' be allowed in the 12 July procession, which must have been frustrating for a man whose family business it was to manufacture such items.

As well as his interest in the Orange Order, W. J. Locke played his part in local politics and was on the Urban Council of Portadown. It was also Bro. Locke who introduced that great Ulster leader, Colonel Edward James Saunderson, to North Armagh. Indeed, Saunderson held Locke in the highest esteem but was unable to attend his funeral in August 1905 due to ill health. A staunch member of St Mark's Parish Church, W. J. Locke was buried after a huge Orange funeral in the family burying ground at Drumcree. His lasting memorial is Carleton Street Orange Hall in which a superb portrait of Bro. W. J. Locke JP hangs.

William Henry Wright (DM 1905–26)

A member of LOL 40, which was later renamed in his memory, W. H. Wright took over the leadership of Portadown District on the death of Bro. W. J. Locke in October 1905 and for the next 21 years he proved more than equal to the high office bestowed upon him. A solicitor by profession, W. H. Wright was born and grew up in the townland of Mullavilly, where he lived with his sisters. He attended the local Church of Ireland church and was a devoted member of the congregation, serving at various times as churchwarden, nominator, synodsman and member of the vestry.

In his professional capacity as town solicitor, W. H. Wright was held in particularly high esteem. He always maintained a high standard of honour and enjoyed the respect and confidence of everyone who knew him. He was at one time legal advisor to Portadown Urban Council as well as Lurgan Rural Council and he also had a large clientele among the commercial and farming community in the town and surrounding area.

As District Master of Portadown, Bro. Wright enjoyed to a marked degree, the affectionate regard of the rank and file, who recognised him as a worthy leader. It was stated that in the whole jurisdiction of the Grand Orange Lodge of Ireland there 'was not a more efficient District Master than Bro. Wright'. His counsel was also valued by members of the Grand Orange Lodge of Ireland and the County Grand Lodge.

Bro. Wright was involved in many aspects of the local community and was the Honorary Secretary of the North Armagh Unionist Association in which capacity he was often called upon to make speeches as part of any platform party. He also played a leading role in the formation and development of the Ulster Volunteers in 1912–14. A well known temperance advocate, he was the president of the local branch of the Catch-My-Pal Society.

By 1926, in his 66th year Bro. Wright, who remained a bachelor, had been suffering from a serious illness which was ultimately to cost him his life on 10 April 1926. He died suddenly at his home in Mullavilly with his sisters in attendance, and was buried in Mullavilly churchyard.

Major David Graham Shillington DL, MP (DM 1926–44)

David Graham Shillington was born on 10 December 1872, the son of Thomas Shillington of Tavanagh House and was educated at Methodist College and then at Rydalmount, Colwyn Bay. After his studies he entered the family business which is still in existence to this day at Shillington's Quay, on the banks of the River Bann. In 1895 Bro. Shillington married Miss Louisa Collen of Killycomain House. They had three children. During the Home Rule crisis of 1912–14 David Shillington was one of the organisers of the Portadown Battalion of the Ulster Volunteer Force. When war broke out he gained a commission in the 9th Battalion Royal Irish Fusiliers (Armagh, Monaghan and Cavan Volunteers) and later attained the rank of major.

Bro. Shillington was involved in local politics and served as the Ulster Unionist Party MP for Central Armagh in the Stormont Parliament. After the resignation of J. M. Andrews as Minister of Labour in 1937, Major Shillington succeeded him in the post. He occupied this position until ill health forced his retirement in 1941. In leading a fully active life Major Shillington was involved in every aspect of society in Portadown and further afield. He was President of the Portadown Branch of the Royal British Legion; President of the town's music festival; a former patron of Portadown Football Club and a director of the Portadown Loan Company.

The funeral of the late Bro. Shillington DL, MP was a private affair and took place from his home in Craigavad to Thomas Street Methodist Church on 25 January 1944. The remains of the late District Master of Portadown District LOL 1 were interred in Drumcree Cemetery.

Dr George Dougan DL, MP (DM 1944–55)

Dr George Dougan became District Master of Portadown District LOL 1 in 1944 following the death of Major D. G. Shillington. He brought with him a wealth of experience of the workings of District Lodge having served under the late. Bro. Shillington for a number of years as District Treasurer. Wor. Bro. Dougan belonged to the Prince of Wales LOL 56.

Dr Dougan was widely known and respected by all sections of the community in the Portadown area, having contact with them through his profession as a general practitioner. As a young man he joined his father's medical practice in Portadown after graduating at Trinity College, Dublin. A keen sportsman he quickly became involved in the local sporting scene as an enthusiastic and experienced oarsman with Portadown Boat Club and, in later years, as a member of Portadown Golf Club serving for a period as captain.

Dr Dougan, like his father before him, had a close association with the Church of Ireland, particularly at the parish of Portadown (St Mark's).

During the First World War Dr Dougan

served with the Royal Army Medical Corps and due to this involvement he continued throughout his life to be a keen supporter of the cause of all ex-servicemen.

The Second World War saw his close involvement with the St John Ambulance Brigade and like many other families at the time he was to share in the grief of the loss of a loved one when one of his sons, Major Hampton Dougan died while on active service with the Royal Army Medical Corps. Also, during the war, when Carleton Street Orange Hall was being used as a billet for the visiting Welsh troops Dr George Dougan made available a room for the use of Orange meetings in his home at Church Street, Portadown.

Wor. Bro. Dougan was one of those belonging to the professional classes who oversaw the running of Portadown District during the post war period, a time of continued expansion of the Order in an atmosphere of peace and confidence.

Described as a quiet gentleman, Wor. Bro. Dougan was nonetheless capable of holding his own in debate, and governed the District in a no-nonsense, brisk and efficient manner. On a Saturday night, when dances were being held in Carleton Street Orange Hall, he frequently would have walked the short distance from his house at Church Street to the hall to ensure all was progressing well and to have a chat with whoever would have been present. Satisfied that all was well, Dr George would quietly leave and return to his home.

During his period as District Master, in the late 1940s, it was proposed in the District Lodge that a band should be booked to provide musical accompaniment when the District would be attending annual Orange church services. Hitherto, the District brethren had walked to such services without a band and unaccompanied by music. The proposal was accepted although a number of the assembled brethren, including the District Master, were apprehensive that the addition of music would lead to a lowering of the solemnity and dignity of church parades.

At the time of his death on 7 April 1955, Wor. Bro. Dougan DL, MP had, by his life of service, gained the respect of the community both locally and abroad. Many tributes were paid to the role he had played in his profession, the Orange Order, the church, the local community and in politics as a Member of Parliament for Central Armagh.

Robert John Magowan OBE, JP (DM 1955–68)

R. J. Magowan's life was marked by the service he gave not only to the Orange Order, but also to the town in which he was born. A diminutive figure, R. J. had unlimited bounds of energy and was a true ambassador for the Orange Institution. Everywhere he went he was affectionately known as Bob.

After joining the Orange Order, Bob became Worshipful Master of Clounagh LOL 9, at the age of 23. He held this position from 1917–19. Soon afterwards he transferred to Edenderry LOL 322 where he was to remain for the rest of his life. He became secretary of the lodge in 1920 and four years later was elected WM. Bob Magowan held this position, except for the period 1929–33, until his death on 12 March 1968. Following his death LOL 322 decided to perpetuate the memory of their late WM by changing the name of the lodge to the R. J. Magowan Memorial Temperance.

R. J. Magowan's name was synonymous with Orangeism not only in his native County of Armagh but also throughout Northern Ireland. He served as District Master of Portadown for fourteen years and was also County Grand Master of Armagh for twenty years. He was elected to the position of Deputy Grand Master of the Grand Lodge of Ireland. Bob also had an abiding interest in the Junior Orange and was instrumental in forming Edenderry Junior LOL 51 in 1927.

In the Royal Black Institution Bob was Deputy Grand Master of the Grand Black Chapter of the British Commonwealth and WM of Portadown District Chapter Number 5. He was in addition Master of his own Royal Black Preceptory, RBP 80, from its inception in 1938.

On 12 July 1961 R. J. performed the opening ceremony of the Orange Museum at Sloan's House in Loughgall, the birthplace of Orangeism. He was instrumental in establishing the museum, collecting Orange relics and maintaining contact with brethren from all around the world.

His service to the Orange Order was only equalled by the public service he gave to the town of his birth, Portadown. He was elected to the Urban Council in 1926 and continued membership until his retirement from public life in 1964. Elected as vice-chairman in 1941–42, he became chairman in 1943 a post he held until the Urban Council was superseded by a Borough Council, when the town received its Charter of Incorporation in 1947. Bob Magowan had the honour of becoming the first Mayor of the Borough and served the town well during his tenure of office. In 1948 Bob Magowan was presented with his portrait in oils in recognition of his services to the Borough of Portadown. The painting, financed by public subscription, was donated by Bob to the Borough Council for safe keeping and now hangs in Portadown Town Hall. Another accolade was soon bestowed on the diminutive figure of Bob Magowan when he was awarded the OBE in the New Year's Honours list of 1949.

Associated for many years with the engineering firm, Portadown Foundry, he worked diligently to bring further employment and new industries to the town.

In 1950–51 he served as Deputy Mayor before again being elected Mayor the following year. The year 1956 saw Bob becoming the first person to be granted the Freedom of Portadown. It was a distinction which probably gave him more pleasure than any other honour bestowed on him. After his death, on 12 March 1968, many tributes were paid to the late R. J. Magowan by those who knew him from both inside and outside the Orange Institution. He was described as 'Honest Bob' because of his total honesty and integrity in all his dealings with everyone he met.

An ardent Methodist, Bob Magowan worshipped in Edenderry Methodist Church, taking a keen interest and supporting role in all aspects of that church's work.

Three years after his death a new shopping and office complex was named the Magowan Buildings in his memory. The opening ceremony was performed by the Rt.

Hon. A. B. D. Faulkner, the Minister of Development, on 9 February 1971. One month later, Brian Faulkner, as he was better known, became the last Prime Minister of Northern Ireland.

Herbert Whitten JP, MP
(DM 1968–1981)

The death of Bro. Herbert Whitten in December 1981 was the end of an era – the Whitten era. A quiet spoken Presbyterian he made his own unique contribution to the glorious annals of Portadown District LOL 1. Herbert Whitten loved the Orange and Royal Black Institutions with a deep intensity and no District officer in Ireland had a closer identification with the grassroots of the loyal orders. From joining the Orange Order as a young man, he was a tireless worker for the cause and served his own private lodge LOL 40 with distinction in various offices.

But it was his elevation to the top office in the District which enabled him to bring his own brand of leadership and it was strong and uncompromising. Bro. Whitten was a man who did not suffer fools gladly, and there were those who would argue that his authoritarian style of leadership was not the type which encouraged free and easy debate. However, he had the gift of being able to get to the heart of a problem, with a minimum of fuss, and while he always gave every man a fair hearing, he did not belong to the school of thought which held that everyone in the lodge room should get up and make lengthy pronouncements on a subject. Once he had seized up the mood of a meeting and the majority feeling Bro. Whitten was soon calling for a vote and getting on with the next item on the agenda.

Quarterly meetings of the district during his term of office, except in the latter years when the 'Troubles' had cast their shadow over things, were generally over at a respectable hour, and brethren were able to sit down to a meal after the election of officers, listen to speeches and still be home by 11 o'clock. One of the secrets of Herbert Whitten's leadership was the fact that he knew practically every single member of the 32 lodges in the District by their Christian names and he also usually knew their families as well! This was due to the fact that he rarely missed an evening in Carleton Street Orange Hall. He not only attended his own private lodge meetings diligently but made it his practice of calling into the other lodges for a chat as well. There was scarcely a night, apart from Sundays, that he did not call into the Orange hall, even if it was only to chat to the boys playing snooker.

Bro. Whitten's interest in all the 32 lodges of Portadown District was acknowledged and in fact was a byword. Each Twelfth night after the parade was over he made it his business to travel around as many lodges as possible to thank them personally for their support and decorum on parade. His travels took him to every Orange Hall in town and those in the outlying country areas as well.

The death of Bro. R. J. Magowan in 1968 created a tremendous void in Orangeism in Portadown District and it speaks volumes for Bro. Whitten's qualities that he was able to step in and maintain the already high standards set by his predecessor. The early years of Bro. Whitten's leadership was marked by steady progress within the District with membership increasing and Portadown enjoying an enormously high reputation within the Institution. The following year saw the beginnings of the civil strife which created strains and tensions throughout the whole community. The Protestant and Unionist population was convulsed by the tensions and the increasing divisions within Unionism. These attacks on Unionism at every level created another challenge for Bro. Whitten who felt it was time for people to stand up and be counted. He offered himself up for election, even though he had never intended to become involved in politics, choosing instead to oversee the running of the family business, Armagh Road Presbyterian Church and of course, the loyal Institutions.

The esteem in which Bro. Whitten was held was manifested by the magnificent response by voters who enabled him to top the poll in the Council election and to be returned with ease to Stormont as Ulster Unionist MP for Central Armagh. Bro. Whitten was elected Mayor of Portadown and later of the new Borough of Craigavon. He also made a considerable impact at Stormont with his calm and compelling arguments during these difficult times.

The 'Troubles' brought violence to Portadown on an unparalleled scale with rioting, shootings, bombings and intimidation. These were difficult times for many Portadown families and Bro. Whitten worked night and day to help people who had housing or other problems caused by intimidation or threats. The year 1972 was one of the most serious of the 'Troubles' and Bro. Whitten showed his qualities of steel on the morning of 12 July of that year. Serious rioting on the morning of the District church parade to Drumcree resulted in part of the parade route in Obins Street being littered with burnt out vehicles. There were rumours that the parade might have to be rerouted or even abandoned, but Bro. Whitten held crucial talks with police and army chiefs and on his return to Carleton Street was able to inform the 1,500 Orangemen that the parade was going ahead.

This was just one example of his firm and decisive leadership during these difficult years and Bro. Whitten's influence was instrumental in preventing things from being even worse.

Bro. Whitten's death in December 1981 was a severe blow to the Orange Institution generally and especially in Portadown where he was universally mourned by every Brother and Sir Knight. Herbert Whitten had followed in the footsteps of a great District Master and had proved more than equal to the task – truly one of the great District Masters in the history of Portadown Orangeism.

John Brownlee (DM 1982–85)

Bro. John Brownlee or Jackie as he is often referred to has given over fifty years of unstinting and devoted service to the Orange Institution. In January 1995 he received his fifty-year service jewel from the present District Master, Bro. Harold Gracey in recognition of his long, loyal and dedicated membership of Edenderry LOL 322, which he joined in 1945. Bro. Brownlee has held many offices both in his own lodge, including that of secretary and treasurer, and at District and County level. In 1977 he was elected treasurer of Portadown District after the murder of Bro. Walker Whitten by the INLA and was also secretary of Carleton Street Orange Hall Committee which undertook many projects to improve the facilities of the hall. An abiding love for the Junior Orange Institution was instilled in the young John Brownlee and in later years he went on to become District Master of Portadown Junior Orange District – a position he held for thirty years. Bro. Brownlee was also Junior County Grand Master for twenty years.

A strongly committed evangelical Christian, Bro. Brownlee is a member of the Kirk Session of Hill Street Presbyterian Church in Lurgan. He has also given sterling service to the youth movement for many years, being a member of the Seagoe Company of the Church Lads Brigade and of the Seagoe Pipe Band of which he was Band Sergeant for thirteen years and Company Quartermaster Sergeant for seven years. This band often accompanied Edenderry LOL 322 and many members of the band passed into the ranks of the lodge.

Noted for his organising ability Bro. Brownlee was one of the officers who planned the highly successful visit of the Belfast Royal Black District Chapter for their 'Last Saturday' demonstration in 1980, the first time the city Sir Knights had been in Portadown for twenty-two years. He was also to the forefront in organising the County Armagh Orange demonstration in Portadown in 1982.

The death of Bro. Whitten in December 1981 left a deep void in Orangeism in Portadown District but the election of Bro. Brownlee to the position of District Master brought a man capable of a high degree of organisational skills. Hard work was something that he had never shirked and in any position of responsibility he had held, Bro. Brownlee always gave of his utmost. In his inaugural message to the members of Portadown District he called on more rank and file members to be prepared to put their 'shoulders to the wheel' and work for the good of the Institution.

In view of his untiring work and commitment to the Institution it is regrettable that Bro. Brownlee's tenure of office was overshadowed by events totally out of his jurisdiction and over which he had no control. Bro. Brownlee should have been able to enjoy a long, peaceful and rewarding tenure as District Master, a position in which he would have excelled, given his love of the Institution and the respect in which he was held. However, the signing of the Anglo-Irish Agreement and the re-routing of traditional parades away from Obins Street, at the behest of the Eire government, created major problems for Portadown District. This affected the District Master in particular as he was the man who had to deal with the problem, sometimes without the support he was entitled to expect and receive. It was an unenviable position to be in – no other District Master in the modern history of Portadown District being subject to the pressures that Bro. Brownlee faced during those difficult days. It is a measure of his ability and that of his successor, Bro. Harold Gracey, that despite all the difficulties endured over those two years, Portadown District has remained intact.

Tragically, Bro. John Brownlee died after a short illness just a few months after recording these details. The authors wish to respectfully dedicate this passage to the memory of a dedicated Orangeman who worked tirelessly in promoting the cause of Orangeism in County Armagh and further afield.

Harold Gracey (1986–To Date)

Harold Gracey became the thirty-first District Master of Portadown District LOL 1 when he was installed to that office in January 1986. He became District Master at a time when Portadown was suffering one of the most unsettled periods in its history due to the re-routing controversy. Many would suggest that it was due to Bro. Gracey's quiet efforts, over a prolonged period, that the issue was finally accommodated. Bro. Gracey, with his innate modesty, would seek to question this notion and would place emphasis on the efforts of his District officers and the common sense of the brethren of Portadown in resolving the issue.

The young Harold Gracey became involved in the Orange Institution at the age of seven, due to the influence of his uncle,

Albert Greenaway who was a member of Edenderry LOL 322 and a District as well as County Grand Lecturer. Harold joined Edenderry Junior LOL 51 and remained a member until the age of sixteen when he became eligible to join the senior organisation. He joined Wingfield Verner's Crimson Star LOL 25 which sat in Carleton Street Orange Hall. Harold explains that it would most probably have been expected that he should join LOL 322 on account of his uncle Albert Greenaway, but at that time many of his friends were joining LOL 25 and so he followed suit.

On entering LOL 25 it was not long before Harold became involved in lecturing. In 1954 he received his Lecturer Certificate from the then District Master, Dr George Dougan, and the following year Bro. Gracey attained his Arch Purple Certificate. He became First Lecturer in his private lodge and a number of years later was elevated to the position as District Lecturer, an office previously held by his uncle, Albert Greenaway. It was in this role as a lecturer, visiting the various lodges of the District, that Bro. Gracey became well known and respected by the brethren.

When asked how he felt, in 1985, about being proposed to this high office, Harold replied, with his usual candour, that at that time he had no idea he would be proposed and certainly had no notion that he would be accepted. However, what the brethren of the district had already recognised was his ability to listen and allow opportunity for the other person to put forward his point of view. This skill, coupled with a calm approach and a desire to keep in close contact with all the brethren prompted his election as District Master.

During the tercentenary year of 1990 Bro. Gracey received further recognition of his services to lecturing when he was elected Deputy County Grand Lecturer for Armagh Grand Orange Lodge.

When asked what he feels he has achieved in Portadown District LOL 1 during his period as District Master he gives one of his characteristic smiles and comments that that is for others to make a judgment. When pressed Harold replies that he would hope he has helped lodges build up a confidence in themselves, as he has undoubtedly built up his own aura of confidence over the ten years he has been in office. Bro. Gracey expresses satisfaction that District membership has remained in a steady state with clear signs that membership is once again on the increase despite the many modern day distractions and leisure activities available to young people. Harold, however, sounds an air of caution warning that members and lodges must not become complacent on the need to continue to recruit members. Due to his lecturing background, Bro. Gracey says that he would like to see lodges place increased emphasis on the ritual of the Order, as he considers that without firmly based ritual the high principles of the Order can become diluted.

Bro. Gracey has already put his mark on the District Lodge by encouraging members to become involved and aware of its workings by emphasising that everyone has an important and integral part to play in the running of the District.

Looking towards the future Harold says that he would like to see this continue and for the Orange Institution, as a whole and Portadown District LOL 1 in particular to grow in stature. When put the question what, in the future he would like to be remembered for, he again refers to the influence of his uncle Albert Greenaway and quotes his yardstick by which future generations can measure someone's contribution 'that no matter what organisation you belong to, when you depart, others can say that you left it a little better. If future Orangemen can say that about my involvement with Portadown District, then I would be happy'.

A member of the Church of Ireland, Bro. Harold Gracey worships at Seagoe Parish Church.

XIV

Carleton Street Orange Hall

PERHAPS one of the most impressive buildings in Portadown and tangible symbols of Orangeism in the area is to be found in Carleton Street in the form of the Orange hall. Carleton Street Orange Hall is one of six halls in Portadown, the others being: Edenderry, Corcrain, Clounagh, Seagoe and Levaghery. It is however by far the largest catering for the needs of twenty-five lodges and preceptories as well as Apprentice Boys' Clubs, Women's and Junior Orange Lodges and also Unionist Associations. The Orange hall in Carleton Street is in fact one of the most famous halls in the Province, being equally as well known in Orangeism as Clifton Street, Sandy Row or Ballymacarrett Orange Halls in Belfast; or Brownlow House in Lurgan.

The Origins of the Hall

The foundation stone for the Orange hall was laid on the present site on 16 January 1873 by Baroness von Stieglitz. She was a member of the well known Blacker family, being the sister of Major Stewart Blacker and the niece of the late Lt.-Col. William Blacker, both of whom were Orange stalwarts in Portadown. The building commenced at a time when Orange halls were virtually unheard of with most Orange lodges holding meetings in private houses or in rooms set aside for that purpose in local hotels or inns. Although the hall was declared open on 12 August 1875, some two years later, much of the work still had to be completed. The unfortunate removal to Liverpool of the Rev. W. Devenish – a prime mover at the beginning of the building project – caused much of the construction work to be temporarily suspended for the next few years.

It was not until 1881 that a special committee, under the chairmanship of the Worshipful District Master, Bro. Joseph McCaughey, was set up and under his guidance this committee saw the building project through to its conclusion. Further emphasis for the completion of the hall came with the tragic death of Major Stewart Blacker, with those responsible wanting it to be completed in his honour. The building work was carried out by Messrs. Collen Bros. of Portadown at a total cost of £1,500. As the work neared completion the following report was to be found in the *Portadown News* dated 31 December 1881:

THE ORANGE HALL – The Orange Hall is approaching completion. One lodge room is now fully fitted up and wainscotting etc. has been added to the others. In a short time a caretaker will be placed in charge of the building: and with the addition of a staircase, the largest hall will be accessible and ready for the reception of an audience. Subscriptions in aid of the work are being received weekly, and more are yet needed to complete the work.

The grand opening of the completed hall took place on 10 April 1882 and it was recorded in the local newspaper that there was a large attendance of brethren from the twenty-six lodges in the District.

Throughout the building project substantial contributions towards the cost were made by Major Stewart Blacker and his sister, the former Hester Anne Blacker, the widow of the Baron von Stieglitz of Bohemia. Mrs Carleton, whose family gave their name to Carleton Street and later to the Carleton Maternity Home, also gave generous financial support. Despite all the fund raising and donations a shortfall of £40 still remained following the opening. However, the Baroness organised a bazaar and the resultant proceeds cleared off all the outstanding debts.

More Years of Expansion

The growing membership of the Orange Order within Portadown District led to the hall quickly becoming inadequate for the needs of the brethren just a few years after it had been completed. In 1888 a number of Orange brethren commenced a reading room under the name of the Portadown Workmen's Reading Room. This work and some additional expansion was soon taken over by the Hall Committee.

A further successful bazaar was held in 1907 to help raise funds towards these improvements. The princely sum of £1,200 was spent on this building work with Messrs. Collen Bros. again carrying out the contract to the specifications which had been drawn up by Mr J. W. Walby, a local architect. This phase of construction work was to give the hall its present distinctive outside appearance. An extension was added to the front of the original building which had been initially set back further from the road.

The newly enlarged hall was formally opened by the Worshipful District Master, Bro. W. H. Wright, on 24 May 1909. Following the official opening ceremony a concert and dance was held in the Orange hall. A motion conveying the sincere thanks of the District to all who had helped in the renovation work was proposed by Bro. Reverend W. H. Towley-Tilson and seconded by Sir Knight R. H. Bell, Worshipful District Master of Portadown Royal Black Chapter.

The 1920s

Stirring and momentous times in the troubled period of the early 1920s saw Carleton Street Orange Hall become the hub of activity in the drive to defeat the IRA in its bid to overthrow the new State of Northern Ireland. The hall was requisitioned by the authorities as a base for the 'A' class Ulster Special Constabulary and during the period 1920–22 the sight of the armed Specials leaving from the hall in their armed Lancia cars to carry out patrols in the town and surrounding countryside was a familiar one.

The caretaker of the hall during this historic time was the famed Mrs Elizabeth Rowe. Known to all loyalists as Liza Rowe, this formidable lady epitomised the spirit of Ulster, completely dedicated to the Orange and Protestant cause. She worked unceasingly for the Orange Institution throughout the 1920s and '30s and after peace had returned her influence in the hall and its affairs was significant.

World War Two

During the Second World War Carleton Street Orange Hall was requisitioned by the military authorities to be used as accommodation for soldiers stationed in the town. Members of Welsh regiments, amongst them the 133rd Field Regiment and the Radnorshire Regiment were billeted in the numerous rooms of the hall. Showers were installed on the ground floor, the black and white tiles of which are still *in situ* in the corridor leading to the Billiard Room. These facilities were strictly for officers only, whose headquarters was located a short distance away in High Street, in the building now occupied by the First Trust Bank.

The lodges which normally held meetings in the hall were granted the use of Dr George Dougan's spacious accommodation a few yards away in Church Place. The District Lodge held its quarterly meetings in Edenderry Orange Hall for most of the duration of the war. Towards the end of the war Carleton Street Orange Hall became the venue for Friday and Saturday night dances which were very popular with the American forces stationed in and around the town. The Yanks even brought their own bands which played in the ballroom. These dances culminated in victory celebrations held in May 1945.

The Fifties and Sixties

In the 1950s and '60s, before today's entertainments of computer games, videos and colour television, Carleton Street Orange Hall was the focal point for the community. Guest teas, concerts and film shows were regular features which were always guaranteed large audiences. Perhaps the most popular form of entertainment were the weekly Saturday night dances, to which people travelled from near and far. On occasions Sunday church services were held in the hall by various denominations at times when refurbishment or redecoration work was being carried out in local churches. The

Billiard Hall was once a regular meeting place for many young men, providing an introduction to the games of snooker and billiards, long before the former was made popular on our television screens.

In the following years various further improvements and refurbishments have been made to the hall. In the 1960s a substantial extension was made to the main function room, doubling it in size and increasing other facilities.

The Centenary Celebrations

In August 1975 Carleton Street Orange Hall celebrated its centenary. A week of events took place incorporating a drumming match, concerts, a fashion show and a religious service which took place on the Sunday afternoon. This week of celebrations culminated with a huge Orange parade through Portadown on Saturday 16 August. The lodges of the District, including Women's and Juniors' took part. To symbolise the coming together of the lodges in Portadown for which Carleton Street is the focal point, lodges left from four different points in the town – Edenderry, Edgarstown, Armagh Road and Tandragee Road – to converge on the District Headquarters. Speakers included the Rev. Martin Smyth, Grand Master and the Rev. Tom Taylor of Tynan. Included in the platform party was the late Bro. Harold McCusker, who had just recently been elected as the MP for Armagh, and of course the Worshipful District Master of Portadown District Bro. Herbert Whitten JP. Following the rally in Carleton Street the full parade made its way from Church Street, to Brownstown Road, West Street and the town centre to Edenderry before returning to Carleton Street where the proceedings terminated.

Following the centenary celebrations of the hall in 1975 a ground floor room, which had formerly been part of the caretaker's residence, was refurbished. This room was officially opened on 22 January 1976 by the Worshipful District Master, Bro. Herbert Whitten JP, and given the title of 'The Centenary Room'.

As the hall passes 120 years of age, refurbishment and maintenance work continues to be given a high priority. Today this task is

overseen by an active and hard-working Hall Renovation Committee. Evidence of this group's vital work is clearly visible as they ensure that Carleton Street Orange Hall is worthy of not only being the flagship of Portadown District, but also as one of the premier facilities of its kind in the Province.

A Sense of History

During the 120 years of Carleton Street Orange Hall's existence, many momentous historical events have occurred within our Province and of course further afield which are worthy of passing note within these pages. This will help give us a sense of perspective not easily brought to mind when one thinks about a building as purely a structure of brick and stone.

At the opening of Carleton Street Orange Hall in 1875 Queen Victoria had already reigned for thirty-eight years, Ireland was united under the British Crown, and Britain was a mighty world power with a vast empire on which it was said 'the sun would never set'. Oh how times have changed! The brethren who had had the foresight to construct the impressive building could never have foreseen that a few years later Irish nationalists would achieve part of their aim in breaking away from the United Kingdom. However, due to the courage of Sir Edward Carson's Ulster Volunteer Force and the sacrifice of the men of the 36th (Ulster) Division, the Ulster Special Constabulary and the RUC, Ulster remained firmly within the jurisdiction of the Crown. This position was further enhanced during the Second World War when Ulster played a key role in securing victory for the Allies.

Since the war Britain has been relegated to a second rate world power with an ever decreasing influence in world affairs. Ulster having remained loyal and having withstood twenty-five years of murderous ethnic cleansing by the Provisional IRA and other republican terrorists, has still maintained her cherished position within the UK. Today the assault by the so-called Pan-Nationalist Front on the Ulster people's democratic wish to remain firmly within the Union is more subtle but no less dangerous.

During all this time Carleton Street Orange Hall has figured in many of the important occasions in Ulster and Unionist history. Great stalwarts such as Edward Carson and James Craig visited the hall during the Home Rule crisis of 1912–14 and during the early years of the Northern Ireland state. Northern Ireland Prime Ministers such as Lord Brookeborough and Captain Terence O'Neill have given speeches at the hall as have many of the leading Unionist figures of the past twenty-five years.

The Grand Lodge of Ireland has held its half-yearly meetings in Carleton Street on a number of occasions, most notably in 1922 when delegates from all the Orange Districts met in the hall after the Order was forced to vacate its Dublin Headquarters as a result of civil unrest brought about by the Irish Civil War. It was at this meeting that the decision was made to relocate the Irish Headquarters of the Orange Order north of the border where it eventually made its home on the Dublin Road in Belfast. Many thought that the Order, given its roots, should have opted for a building in County Armagh, with the consensus of opinion opting for Portadown. If that decision had been made Carleton Street may have become, not only the headquarters for the Orange Order in Portadown, but also of the whole of Ireland.

Focal Point

Although Portadown narrowly missed out on becoming the headquarters of the Orange Institution, Carleton Street Orange Hall remains as the focal point of Orangeism in the area. It is of course a hive of activity on the big occasions in the loyalist calendar. Each 12 July it is the rallying point for the thirty-two lodges of Portadown District LOL 1 as they converge from various parts of the town. The same is also true for the 13 July, when the nineteen Preceptories of the Royal Black Institution also meet at Carleton Street to begin their day of celebrations which culminates in the famous Sham Fight at Scarva. Derry Day celebrations of the Apprentice Boys also begin at the Orange Hall.

On other occasions such as 'Black' Saturday, the hall has been crowded with Sir Knights from Belfast, as visiting preceptories use the building for meals and other events. Belfast Districts first visited the town in 1923 for their August demonstrations and they have made return visits on a number of other occasions. Carleton Street has played a key role in accommodating thousands of visitors from the city.

As Portadown District LOL 1 celebrates its Bicentenary, Carleton Street Orange Hall stands proudly as the headquarters of the Orange Order in the area. Due to its location it has fortunately been able to escape the malicious assaults that have been made against many other Orange halls, particularly those situated at interfaces with nationalist/republican areas.

Carleton Street Orange Hall has remained a vibrant centre and symbol of Orangeism during a period which has been one of the most difficult in the history of Orangeism in the Province. It is a tribute to the officers of the District and the members of the hall committees throughout its history, that Carleton Street Orange Hall has kept pace with the demands made of it through the years.

XV

Histories of Private Lodges

LOL 7 Breagh Leading Heroes

WARRANT No. 7 does not appear on the list left by James Sloan of the warrants he signed on the 21 September 1795, however, the records show that by August 1796 the lodge was sitting at Scots Street with John McCreery as Master. In Sibbett's *History of Orangeism* and Wolsey's *Orangeism in Portadown District* it is recorded that:

> Mr. Thomas Lecky, of Breagh, a most determined leader, who charged the rebel position at the Battle of the Diamond, obtained No 7, which afterwards went to Portadown District. According to tradition, he owed this good fortune to his persistent flourishing of a blackthorn stick over the heads of those assembled in Mr. Sloan's parlour.

In 1829 the Master of the lodge was recorded as Bartley Robinson and at the same time a duplicate warrant was issued to County Antrim, Belfast. By 1847 the No. 7 at Portadown District had become known as Leganny Orange Lodge, the warrant to be renewed in 1850 with Wilson Crockett as Master and renewed a further time in 1887 now under the title of Richmount Temperance LOL.

The lodge was to settle with the building of its own Orange hall at Breagh in 1891 but prior to this the lodge is recorded as sitting at Diviney in July 1887 before moving to Breagh in October 1887.

In 1932 the lodge unfurled a banner featuring King William crossing the Boyne on the front and the 'Secret of England's Greatness' on the reverse. These scenes were repeated on the lodge's next banner which was unfurled in 1954. The lodge's next banner, featuring King William crossing the Boyne on the front, and the Biblical scene of 'My faith Looks Up To Thee' on the reverse, was unfurled at a ceremony held on 21 May 1971.

During the 'Troubles' the lodge was to suffer the loss of Bro. Alfred Doyle, a sergeant in the Ulster Defence Regiment who, along with two friends, was brutally murdered by republican terrorists on 3 June 1975. The three men had been returning home from a dog show in the Irish Republic when their car was ambushed on the border near Killeen, County Armagh.

The late Bro. Isaac G. Hawthorne JP, MP who died in December 1992 served as Worshipful Master of the lodge from 1956–58. Bro. Hawthorne was a former MP for Central Armagh and also a former Chief Whip in the Northern Ireland Parliament at Stormont.

Members of LOL 7 unfurled a new banner in June 1995. The banner, featuring a depiction of Jesus walking on the water and a portrait of King William III, was unfurled by Mrs Sommerville whilst the dedication ceremony was performed by the Reverend John Pickering. Also in attendance was Bro. David Trimble MP for Upper Bann.

Worshipful Masters of LOL 7 from 1935 are as follows:

1935–43	David Carrick
1943–49	David Boseman
1949–54	Isaac Taylor
1954–56	John Henderson
1956–58	Isaac Hawthorne J.P. M.P.
1958–60	David Carville
1960–62	Norman Millsop
1962–78	Henry Eldon
1978–80	Keith Sharpe
1980–84	Herbert Anderson
1984–88	Henry Eldon
1988–90	Kenneth Thornton
1990–	Robert Anderson

LOL 8 Star of Erin, Drumheriff

Following the Battle of the Diamond Richard Robinson, Timnakeel, received the first warrant in the house of James Sloan at Loughgall. In 1796 the lodge was recorded as sitting in Drumheriff. It also sat at Ballyfodrin where in 1829 it had as its Master John Todd. The warrant was renewed to Thomas Crockett WM in 1891 and the lodge was meeting in the house of Samuel McCoo in 1892. The following year, 1893, the lodge was meeting in the house of William Sparkes, Cornamuckley, but by the end of 1900 was again back at Drumheriff. The new Orange hall was erected in 1912 and at the time Samuel Smyth was the lodge's Worshipful Master.

LOL 9 The Earl of Beaconsfield Primrose League, Clounagh

No. 9 first sat at the Grange with John Winter as its Master up to 1815. In 1819 the lodge received authorisation to move to the Dobbin and during the next forty years the lodge was known as the Derryhale or Dobbin lodge depending on its meeting place. By 2 February 1829 the lodge's Master was noted as John Watson. The warrant fell temporarily dormant for some fourteen years but by 1862 it was operative again with Thomas Hoy as its Master. By 1864 the lodge was known as Artabracka LOL and in 1875 had a Master by the name of William Maxwell. 1883 saw a further move to Derryhale where we find the lodge sitting in the house of Mr Ruddell, Drumnasoo.

It was in 1896 that No. 9 assumed the title as The Earl of Beaconsfield Primrose League. By this time the lodge was sitting in Portadown and by 1904, under Worshipful Master, James Uprichard, Clounagh Orange Hall was built.

The late Bro. George Hanlon served with the Royal Navy during the Second World War. He saw service in a number of theatres of operations including the hazardous Arctic convoys bringing supplies to the Russians. Bro. Cecil McKinney also saw service during the war as a member of the Royal Ulster Rifles and Parachute Regiment.

The lodge's current banner, featuring a painting of Benjamin Disraeli, the Prime Minister of the United Kindom during the 1870s, was unfurled in the 1960s.

Clounagh Orange Hall was extensively renovated after a boiler explosion and was reopened in 1988. Many of the lodge's records, including minute books and registers, were lost in the explosion and as a result the information on the lodge is not as detailed as the members would have liked.

LOL 10 Greenisland True Blues, Derrinraw.

In 1796 No. 10 was recorded as sitting at Richmount. During the period 1823 to March 1825 it was also recorded as meeting at Glenanne and up to 1904 in Markethill District. In the year 1829 the Master was recorded as Mark Berry and by 1856 the lodge was sitting at Derryvore with Alex. Trotter as its Master. The place of sitting of the number moved from Kilmore to Derryvane around 1864 before moving to Richmount, Ballyoran, Edgarstown and settling at Derrinraw about 1870. The lodge sat in the house of William McFadden before the Orange hall was built and opened on 16 January 1873. In 1875 Thomas A. Woodhouse was the Worshipful Master of the lodge and the warrant was renewed to John Maguire WM on 12 May 1894. Wolsey noted in his book *Orangeism in Portadown District* that:

> John McNally walked from Derrinraw to the Red Lion to see Robinson Ruddock to get No. 10 warrant. James Taylor, a stone-cutter, cut the stone for the Hall (the oldest in Portadown District) and gave it to the Lodge free of cost.

The hall at Derrinraw, dating from 1873, is thought to be the oldest purpose built Orange hall in County Armagh and because of its unique history, the brethren of LOL 10 are at the moment endeavouring to have the building listed by the DoE Historic Buildings and Monuments Branch. An officer from the DoE has already paid a visit to the hall and is currently compiling a report to be considered by his Department. Unique features of the hall include an original framed portrait of Queen Victoria, a lodge warrant from 1896, a lodge seal, possibly dating from the late 1790s and probably most unique of all – original gaslight fittings within the hall.

LOL 13 The Rising Sons of William, Derrinraw

In 1796 No. 13 was recorded as sitting in Drumcree with John Flavelle as its Master. By 1819 the lodge has moved to Kilmagamish with John Atkinson recorded as Master on 2 February 1829 and it returns to Drumcree in 1844. The Registry of lodges for 1856 names the Master of the lodge as John Abraham during which year it was meeting at Corcrain. In 1875 the lodge was meeting at Derryall with Robert Bird as Master. Having moved to Derrinraw in 1880 the No. 13 warrant was renewed by John Forbes WM on 26 June 1891.

LOL 13, the smallest lodge in the District, is also another of the numerous drumming lodges in Portadown.

LOL 18 Golden Springs, Brackagh

The No. 18 warrant was first recorded as meeting in Portadown in 1796 with Its Worshipful Master as John Lutton. By 1825 the meeting place had moved to Drumnakelly and the Master in 1829 was Arthur Wright. For a number of years from 1838, when the lodge had a membership of twelve brethren, the lodge was meeting in the Mahon area to the extent it became known as the Mahon Lodge. In 1842 it was meeting at the house of Robert Wright, Worshipful Master, at the Mahon. By the year 1860 the lodge had moved to Brackagh meeting in the home of James McKeown. 1875 saw Richard A. Topley as Master and in 1883 the lodge was meeting at John Toal's, Brackagh. The new hall was erected at Brackagh in 1914 and in 1923 Mr and Mrs Maginnis provided an organ for the hall as religious services were held in the hall from time to time. Also, in 1923 a new banner was obtained by LOL 18.

John McIntyre was installed as Worshipful Master in 1933 and assisted by Joseph Hodgen who occupied the deputy chair. Bro. McIntyre occupied the chair until 1942 when Bro. John G. Toal took over as Master.

In 1943 a memorial tablet was erected in Brackagh Orange Hall by the officers and members of LOL 18 and RBP 265 in memory of the Late Sir Knight and Bro. John Toal 1891 to 1942.

Carleton street Orange Hall was the venue for the unfurling and dedication of the lodge's new banner on 10 June 1960.

The unfurling ceremony was performed by Mrs Tom Raymond.

A new banner featuring a painting of King William III on horseback was unfurled on 22 May 1992. The unfurling ceremony was performed by Bro. John Toal, Worshipful Master of LOL 18 and the banner was dedicated by Bro. Reverend Percy Patterson, Deputy Grand Chaplain. The proceedings were chaired by the County Grand Master, Right Wor. Bro. Norman R. S. Hood.

Bro. John G. Toal the Worshipful Master of LOL 18 and Bro. Robert M. Toal, Secretary were presented with Orange Bowls in recognition of fifty years outstanding service in office. Bro. Robert Toal has held the office of Secretary from 1944 to date and is almost certainly the longest serving lodge Secretary within Portadown District.

On 13 October 1993 a tablet was unveiled in memory of the late Sir Knight and Bro. John G. Toal who had served in the office of Worshipful Master from 1942 until 1993, a period of fifty-one years. A video of the 1992 Banner Unfurling and the unveiling of the memorial tablet has been taken. In 1993 Bro. Leslie Wells was installed as Worshipful Master, assisted by Bro. Tom Houston in the deputy chair. Twelve of the present membership of LOL 18 are senior citizens and nine of them have been over fifty years in LOL 18.

Brackagh is one of the major Lambeg drumming lodges within Portadown District.

LOL 19 Ballyworkan Truth Defenders

The first recorded meeting place of No. 19 is at Ballyworkan in 1796 with Arthur Huston as Master. On the 2 February 1829 the Master of the lodge was William Gillespie, and in 1856 the lodge was sitting in Ballyworkan with John Cullen as Master. In the years 1875 and 1891 the Master was recorded as James Miller, Portadown.

Unlike many other lodges of the time No. 19 does not appear to have moved around different parts of the surrounding countryside. In fact, it is noted that the lodge has always met around Whiteside's Hill up to 1923 where, like most other lodges, it met in private houses. In 1923 the house of John Stewart, in which the lodge had met for many years, was purchased and turned into a suitable hall.

In 1937 LOL 19 unfurled a new banner, the ceremony was carried out by Sister Miss N. Wright of Mullavilly, the sister of the late W. H. Wright former District Master of Portadown, with Bro. the Rt. Hon. Major D. G. Shillington DL, MP, District Master, presiding.

During the Second World War Bro. Taylor Tweedie made the Supreme Sacrifice when he was Killed in Action at Monte Casino, Italy.

The lodge's present banner features paintings of the 'Fortunate Escape of King William' and the burning at the stake of Latimer and Ridley. Ballyworkan is another of the many drumming lodges within the District.

The present Deputy District Master, Bro. Roy McMahon is a member of this lodge.

LOL 20 Erin's Royal Standard, Kilmagamish

No. 20 was working under Worshipful Master William Hall at Derryanville in 1796. Membership records show that by 1814 the lodge had thirty-nine members, showing an increase to sixty-six by 1816. In 1819 the lodge was meeting at Kilmagamish and in 1829 the Master was Curran Atkinson. The same year reveals that a duplicate warrant had been issued to Co. Down. In 1856 the lodge was still sitting at Kilmagamish with George Forsythe as Master. By this time three duplicate No. 20 warrants were in circulation, one at Co. Tyrone and two in Co. Down. In 1880 the number had become known as Foy LOL but in 1884 the name was changed to Waterloo Verner Heroes.

The Forsythe family would appear to have had a strong connection with No. 20 as it was recorded in 1874 that the lodge was paying James Forsythe 4d per week for sitting in his room in Foy. Indeed in 1890 the lodge was still meeting at Forsythe's although this time at William Forsythe's at Derrymattery. In the same year the lodge meeting place moved to Mr McFall's in Drumena but only for a short period because the following year 1891 it had moved again this time to the mill in a house of William Forsythe. The year 1893 saw the lodge meeting at Kilmagamish, 1902 at

Corbackey and in 1910 back at George Forsythe's at Kilmagamish. The new Orange hall was opened on 13 September 1913.

Members of the lodge unfurled a new banner on 12 June 1993. The banner features a painting of Drumcree Parish Church on the front and a depiction of King William III landing at Carrickfergus on the reverse. The ceremony, which took place after the Mini Twelfth, was performed by Bro. William Smyth, the oldest member of the lodge. The banner was dedicated by the Reverend Tom Taylor.

Officers of the lodge for 1995 are as follows:

Worshipful Master ... Richard Ruddell
Deputy Master .... William Neill
Secretary .... William Gilmour
Treasurer .... David Boyce
Chaplain .... Samuel Martin

LOL 22 Bocombra True Blues

No. 22 warrant originated in Lurgan District. On 2 February 1829 it was recorded in Lurgan with Henry Dynes as Master. The year 1825 reveals Thomas McDowell as Master and by 1856 the lodge was sitting at Bocombra with Thomas Malcolmson as Master. In the year 1891 Thomas McDowell of Lurgan was again noted as Master of the lodge. Bocombra Orange Hall was opened in 1908.

The lodge transferred to Portadown District in 1992.

Lodge Officers for 1995 are:

Worshipful Master ... Andrew Fletcher
Deputy Master .... Brian Holmes
Secretary .... Paul Holmes
Treasurer .... Thomas Holmes
Chaplain .... Samuel Preston

LOL 25 Wingfield Verner's Crimson Star, Portadown

No. 25 has continually sat in Portadown since 1796. Initially known as The Boyne Club of Loyalists No. 25 the lodge had as its first Master James Dawson. In 1854 the lodge changed its name and became known as the Calimotte Orange Lodge. The Master in 1856 was Thomas Henry and in 1869 the lodge was meeting in the house of John

Williamson at Woodhouse Street. David Clayton, Clounagh, who died in 1927, was for many years chaplain and led the lodge on the Twelfth on his own white horse. Duplicate warrants were issued in Counties Down and Londonderry in 1856.

LOL 25 meets in Carleton Street Orange Hall. Bro. Harold Gracey, the Worshipful Master of Portadown District is a member of this lodge.

LOL 26 Churchview, Seagoe

No. 26 warrant was first issued to Lurgan District in 1798. 2 February 1829 shows the warrant with a Johusa Cherry, Lurgan, and a duplicate with Banbridge District. On the morning of 12 July 1848, LOL 26 was presented with a beautiful stand of colours by Mrs Saurin (née Warburton, the sister of General Warburton, a famous Australian explorer) and the wife of the Reverend James Saurin, the Rector of Seagoe. In 1856 No. 26 was still with Lurgan District and in 1875 Henry McCrory was Master and two duplicates were working in Banbridge. 1891 shows the Master again as Henry McCrory.

In 1897 the foundation stone for a new Orange hall at Seagoe was laid by Baroness Von Stieglitz a member of the well known Blacker family. The Baroness had kindly donated the land on which the Orange hall was to be erected.

In 1972 LOL 26 transferred from Lurgan District LOL 6 to Portadown District LOL 1.

The members of LOL 26 unfurled a new banner, featuring a painting of the nearby Seagoe Parish Church, on 26 June 1992. The chairman for the occasion was Bro. Harold Gracey, District Master. The unfurling ceremony was performed by Mrs A. Magee and the banner dedicated by W. Bro. Reverend Tom Taylor, Deputy County Grand Chaplain. The guest speaker at the meeting was the Ulster Unionist MP for Upper Bann, Bro. David Trimble.

LOL 31 Bible and Crown Defenders, Kilmoriarty

On the 6 August 1796 this warrant was taken out by Abraham Hart with a membership of over fifty. The following year the lodge was meeting at Tottens Hill with Joseph Morrison as Master. During the next period of years the lodge had a number of name changes. In 1813 it was known as the Mullentine Excelsior Lodge and in 1882 became known as Kilmoriarty Excelsior Lodge when John Summerville was Master. A further name change resulted in 1886 to Derry Rossmore Scarlet Star and the final change of name to Bible and Crown Defenders came about in 1905. In 1856 the lodge was meeting at Mullentine with Benjamin Ford as Master and by 1875 the Master was William Lawson. During the 1920s membership of the lodge was up to seventy. Kilmoriarity Orange Hall was opened on Easter Monday 1912.

On 24 May 1985 the members of LOL 31 unfurled a new banner which featured a portrait of their late Worshipful Master, Bro. Tom Woods. The unfurling ceremony was performed by his son, Bro. Tommie Woods.

The Pride of the Birches Accordion Band accompanies LOL 31 on parade.

Bro. Private James Magee of LOL 31 served during the Great War. He was killed in action. The lodge has a photograph of Bro. Magee, in full service uniform, which was taken shortly before he left for the Front.

The lodge's original warrant, issued in 1796, is in the Orange Museum in Loughgall.

The late Bro. W. D. Thompson was lodge Secretary from 1935 until his death in 1978. Bro. Thompson was also District Secretary 1969–78. The present District Secretary, Bro. Robert Wallace, is a member of LOL 31.

In 1994 Kilmoriarty Orange Hall was re-roofed at a cost of £2,300.

Worshipful Masters of the lodge from 1922 are as follows:

1922–50	James Conn
1951–83	T. R. Woods
1984–85	R. J. Hanlon snr.
1986–88	B. Partridge
1989–90	Samuel Ruddell snr.
1991–92	Robert Hall
1993–94	H. E. Browne
1995–	Victor Fleming

LOL 35 St Aiden's True Blues, Kilmore

No. 35 is one of the warrants issued on the day of the Battle of the Diamond to George Innis, Grange, O'Neilland. In 1796 the lodge was still meeting at the Grange with Worshipful Master Richard Robinson but by 1820 it was meeting at Ballywilly. The year of 1856 notes the meeting place as Anahoe and James Pierson as Master. In 1875 John Haughton was Master. On the 24 April 1905, Easter Monday, an Orange hall was opened on a site given by the late Rev. Richard Johnston.

Kilmore Orange Hall was the venue for a double dedication ceremony on 24 April 1992 when members of LOL 35 unfurled a new banner featuring a painting of Kilmore Parish Church and dedicated a new set of officers' collarettes for the lodge. The service was conducted by Reverend E. T. Dundas, assisted by W. Bro. Reverend Tom Taylor, who performed the unfurling and dedication ceremonies.

Worshipful Masters of the lodge since 1940 have included the following brethren:

John Newell	Simon McAlaister
George Millsop	W. G. Ferguson
Thomas Falloon	Joseph Falloon jnr.
William Alderdice	David Newell
Joseph Falloon snr.	Samuel Millsop

The present Worshipful Master is Bro. Herbert Tedford. The District Outside Tyler, Bro. Ian Falloon, is a member of this lodge.

LOL 40 Herbert Whitten Memorial, Portadown

This lodge was formed in 1796 at the Grange as the Erne Temperance LOL, its first Master being Laurence Ruddock. By 1856 it was still meeting at the Grange with Worshipful Master, William Taylor. In 1901 it was meeting in Portadown with W. J. Locke JP Master, also District Master of Portadown District. Following his death in August 1905, a resolution was passed at the September meeting:

That we express our deep sorrow on the death of Br. W. J. Locke W.M. of this Lodge. He was Master of this Lodge during the many years it worked in Portadown, and we always found him to be not only a loyal and earnest fellow-worker but a true and faithful friend. He was greatly attached to the Orange Institution and worked Zealously in its interests and the Institution, and especially our District, will greatly miss him who for so many years has been our tried and trusted friend.

W. H. Wright was secretary of the lodge until his death in 1921. He was also District Master of Portadown District. Following his death the lodge became known as W. H. Wright Memorial. In 1932 Herbert Whitten was elected secretary of the lodge. He also became District Master of Portadown District in 1968. Bro. George Dougan, Worshipful District Master of Portadown from 1944 to 1955, was a member of LOL 40 before his transfer to LOL 56.

After the death of the Worshipful District Master, Bro. Herbert Whitten, the lodge was renamed to perpetuate his memory. In June 1984 a new banner featuring a portrait of the late Bro. Herbert Whitten was unfurled by members of the lodge.

The lodge is accompanied by the Star of David Accordian Band on the Twelfth of July.

Lodge officers for 1995 are as follows:

Worshipful Master ... Tom Jones
Deputy Master .... N. Davison
Secretary .... W. Woods
Treasurer .... Tom Johnston
Chaplain .... Garfield Hyde

LOL 40 meets in Carleton Street Orange Hall.

LOL 56 Prince of Wales, Portadown

No. 56 has never left Portadown District. Thomas Buntin was the first Master of the lodge. On the 1 July 1851 it was decided that the lodge should be called Temperance LOL. In 1856 James White was Master. At the time there were two other LOL 56 warrants operating in Co. Cavan and Co. Londonderry. The Portadown warrant fell dormant during the period 1862–1864 but in 1864 the warrant was reorganised under the name of Prince of Wales with Worshipful Master, Abraham Harvey. In 1870 a presentation was made by the lodge of a bridle and saddle to the Rev. Albert J. Ard, curate of Drumcree, following the presentation of a horse by the parishioners of Drumcree to him. On the 11 July 1878 the lodge name was changed to Portadown Conqueror but in 1883 it reverted back to Prince of Wales. Mention is made of the fact that there was a Prince of Wales Conservative Flute Band. At the 1884 demonstration in Newry LOL 56 was headed by their brass band. The County Grand Master of the time, Sir Edward Wingfield Verner, took the lodge and band out of their place in the procession and put them in front of the County Grand Lodge of Dublin, asking them to lead the entire procession of 40,000 Orangemen through the streets of Newry to the place of meeting at Altnaveigh.

Lodge officers for 1995 are as follows:

Worshipful Master ... W. G. McCabe
Deputy Master .... C. Forbes
Secretary .... W. Miller
Treasurer .... G. Magowan
Chaplain .... C. Huston

LOL 56 meets in Carleton Street Orange Hall.

LOL 58 Colonel Saunderson's Silver Stream, Portadown

From 1796 to 1832 No. 58 sat at Ballinteggart. The first Master of the lodge was James Ferguson. In 1834 the lodge was now sitting at Kilmoriarty with James Ruddell as Master. In the same year a problem seems to have arisen due to a duplicate 58 Warrant. On 3 September the Grand committee of GOLI resolved

...that No. having been originally been given to the first mentioned District and that a duplicate having been illegally trafficked by the other districts resolved that No. 58 Portadown District be the only Lodge acknowledged as sitting under a Warrant of that Number and that all others having that No. to be declared cancelled.

On 2 January 1883 the number was restored after being dormant for a period of time by Joseph McCaghey District Master, and W. J. Locke Deputy District Master. At the time six members were present.

Four members of the lodge served in His Majesty's Forces during World War II. They were Bros. R. J. Whyte, F. Todd, R. H. Bunting and R. J. Jones.

The lodge was renamed after Colonel Edward James Saunderson, a loyal Orangeman and the Unionist MP for North Armagh. The lodge's two previous bannerettes have featured portraits of King William III and Colonel Saunderson. A portrait of Colonel Saunderson is featured on the reverse of the lodge's current bannerette which was unfurled on 18 April 1989. The bannerette was presented to the lodge by members of the Wylie family and features a portrait of the late Bro. R. J. Wylie PM on the front.

Worshipful Masters of the lodge since 1935 are as follows:

1935–38	Thomas Jameson
1939–40	R. J. Wylie
1941–45	Thomas Jameson
1946–55	R. J. Wylie
1956–58	J. Symington
1959	S. McElroy
1960–63	C. D. Carson
1964–68	R. Lynass
1969	A. Major
1970–73	J. Symington
1974	R. Carson
1975	A. Harland
1976–77	W. P. Hanna
1978–80	J. E. Carson
1981–82	C. Smyth
1983–84	R. Carson
1985	J. Symington
1986–87	M. Carson
1988–89	R. J. Watton
1990–91	H. Lappin
1992–93	A. Jenkinson
1994–	P. Harland

LOL 58 meets in Carleton Street Orange Hall.

LOL 78 Bible and Crown Defenders, Derrycarne

In 1796 No. 78 was meeting in Portadown with Miles Atkinson as its Master. In 1809 the number fell dormant for a short time before being taken out again in 1810 with Henry Chamney as Master. He was to remain as Master to 1816 when it again fell dormant. In 1821 the warrant was reopened with William Irwin, the District Secretary becoming Worshipful Master of the lodge. By 1844 the lodge was meeting at

Derrycorey and in 1856 the lodge was now meeting at Derrycarne with Robert Johnston under a new warrant 'The Warrant having been carried off to Australia a renewal was granted 2 February 1849'. In 1890 the lodge was given permission to use the name Bible and Crown Defenders.

The lodge opened a new hall in a ceremony which took place in 1911.

In 1994 two members of the lodge received presentations to mark their 50 years' membership of the lodge. Bro. Samuel Dowd, Worshipful Master of LOL 78 and Bro. Thomas Forbes, his deputy, received 50 year Membership Certificates and inscribed Bibles from the Worshipful District Master Bro. Harold Gracey. Both men joined the lodge as teenagers in 1944.

The current banner of LOL 78 depicts, as their name suggests, a Bible and Crown on the front, whilst on the reverse is depicted the Biblical scene 'My Faith looks up to Thee'.

Recently members of the lodge purchased Derrycarne Primary School as new accommodation for the lodge. The members are now embarking on an ambitious renovation programme for the hall.

Worshipful Masters of the lodge since 1981 are as follows:

1981–91	Noel Jones
1991–92	Carl Cunningham
1992–93	Robert Hyde
1993–	Samuel Dowd

Previous to this Robert Maginn occupied the chair for eight years, whilst before him George Robinson was Worshipful Master of the lodge for twenty years.

LOL 80 Star of the North, Ballylisk

In 1796 the lodge was meeting at Ballyworkan with William Wright as Master but by 1819 the meeting place had moved to Drumnakelly. The year 1856 saw William Mateer as Master with the lodge sitting at Mullahead. In 1829 the warrant was in the name of William Brownlow, Portadown and in 1875 in the name of George Laverty.

Ballylisk Orange Hall was opened on 12 July 1920 when the brethren of LOL 80

played host to the County Armagh demonstration.

In 1938 the lodge unfurled a new banner featuring King William III crossing the Boyne on the front and 'The secret of England's greatness' on the reverse. The ceremony was performed by the Deputy District Master of Bessbrook District, Bro. T. Martin, with Wor. Bro. George A. Locke, Worshipful Master of Portadown Royal Arch Purple Chapter presiding.

The lodge's current banner, which features a depiction of David slaying Goliath, was unfurled in 1975.

To commemorate the 75th anniversary of the opening of Ballylisk Orange Hall, Portadown Orangemen held their quarterly District meeting at the hall on 28 June 1995. The meeting took place during one of the warmest spells of weather experienced in Northern Ireland for over sixty years.

Officers of the lodge for 1995 are as follows:

Worshipful Master ...	W. J. Hamill
Deputy Master	M. W. Henderson
Secretary	W. K. Henderson*
Treasurer	W. K. Henderson
Chaplain	W. Shortt
	(*acting)

LOL 81 Derryhale

Warrant No. 81 first appeared in Portadown District records in 1800 with William Hunniford as Master. In 1856 the lodge was sitting at Derryhale and Robert Anderson was Master. The lodge was still noted at that location in 1875. Prior to the building of its own hall for meetings in 1899 the lodge had met in the houses of John McQuillan, Mullalelish; Hector Teggart, Derryhale; Thomas Tougher, Derryhale; and William McKinney, Lisavague.

On 12 July 1922 the County Armagh demonstration was held at Derryhale on the occasion of the opening of Derryhale Orange Hall.

LOL 89 Rechab's True Blues Total Abstinence, Portadown

No. 89 was meeting in Timnakeel in 1796 with William Dillon as Master. The warrant moved to Portadown in 1820 with Daniel

Bulla becoming Master in 1882. By 1844 the lodge was meeting in Battlehill but the following year the meeting place had moved to Derryhale. In 1856 the Master was Thomas Hoey and at this time the place of sitting was noted as Artabracka. The number was to fall dormant from 1884–1867 when it appears at Cock Hill, Tartaraghan, with William Gardiner as Master. The number was to again have a period when it was dormant from 1884–1889 when William Best of Killycomain became Master. It was in 1893 that the lodge took the name of Rechab's True Blues and had its bye-laws confirmed by the Grand Lodge of Ireland.

W. H. Wolsey, the author of *Orangeism in Portadown District*, was a member of this lodge fulfilling the post of Worshipful Master in 1945 and again in 1953. During World War II the following brethren saw active service in His Majesty's Forces: John Campbell (HMS *Centurion*), Fred Harvey (Royal Air Force), Harry McKerr and C. H. Rock.

In 1943 Bro. R. J. Hewitt was appointed SDC of the Ulster Special Constabulary in Portadown.

Members of the lodge unfurled a new bannerette on 9 July 1958 at Carleton Street Orange Hall. The ceremony was chaired by Bro. Herbert Whitten, whilst the unfurling of the bannerette was performed by Bro. J. Dermott.

In 1959 W. H. Wolsey became Mayor of Portadown, receiving the compliments of LOL 89 for his services to the brethren whilst being a member of the Council.

LOL 89 which sat in Carleton Street Orange Hall became dormant in the late 1980s.

LOL 99 Johnston's Royal Standard, Portadown

The first mention of No. 99 is in 1796 at Clonamola with John Erwin as Master. In the year 1810 the lodge was meeting at Leganny but by 1856 it had moved to Baltylum and had as its Master, Bro. William Weir. During the years 1862–1870 the lodge was known as William Street Orange lodge and its Master was James Albin. By 1874 the lodge was meeting in Obins Street and the Worshipful Master in 1875

was Joseph McCaughey. The number fell dormant for a short period but was revived in 1881 with William Jackson as Master. In 1882 the lodge took the name of Royal Standard which was extended to William Johnston Royal Standard in 1893. At one stage LOL 99 had its own band and Lambeg drums.

In 1937 a new banner was unfurled by Sister Mrs Shillington, the wife of the District Master, with Bro. David Rock MBE, JP presiding over the ceremony. The banner featured a portrait of Lord Carson, who had died in 1935 and a painting of King William III.

William Baxter, Portadown's oldest surviving veteran of the Battle of the Somme, was a member of this lodge. He died in 1993. Bro. Tommy Speers, a Royal Air Force veteran, who took part in the Normandy landings in June 1944, laid the wreath at the town's War Memorial on the occasion of the District's pre-Twelfth Orange parade commemorating the 50th Anniversary of D-Day. Tommy, a Past Master of the lodge died shortly after this event. His son Gordon was installed as Worshipful Master of LOL 99 in January 1995 taking over from his late brother Billy, who had recently occupied the chair until his death in July 1994.

LOL 99 meets in Carleton Street Orange Hall.

LOL 107 Sir Edward Wingfield Verner's True Blues, Knocknamuckly

This warrant was first noted in 1796 sitting at Drumnakelly with Henry Jackson as Master. By 1819 it was sitting at the Dobbin and the following year had moved to Kilmoriarty where William Hyde was Master. The years of 1845 and 1846 saw the lodge sitting at Corcrain and Artabracka, respectively, the latter of which it was to remain at to 1867. In the Registry of 1856 the Master was noted as James Brownlee. The lodge was on the move again in 1868 when it moved to Ballygargan. By the year 1875 a Malcolm Moffet was shown as Master with a duplicate warrant at Markethill District. The title of Verner's True Blues was granted in 1883. The lodge was renamed Sir Edward Wingfield Verner's True Blues on the death of the County Grand Master of Armagh, who was the son of Sir William Verner.

The original hall was opened on 5 November 1894 and destroyed by a terrorist bomb on 28 March 1976. The rebuilt hall was opened on 20 August 1977. The brethren, accompanied by Edgarstown Accordion Band and Crozier Memorial Pipe Band, paraded from Knocknamuckley Parish Church, via Blacker's Mill to the hall. The car park and platform were decorated with bunting and Lambeg drummers were beating out a tune.

The platform party comprised Bro. A. J. Anderson, County Grand Master, Bro. H. Whitten, District Master, Bro. J. H. McCusker MP, Bro. Eric Crozier, Lurgan District Master, Bro. Captain Michael Armstrong, Bro. Rev. A. J. Finch, former rector Knocknamuckley Parish Church, Rev. R. Haskins, Bluestone Methodist Church, Bro. John Toal, WM LOL 18, and Bro. Bob Blair, WM LOL 61.

The chairman Bro. Eric Davison, WM LOL 107, gave details of the history of the warrant and the hall to its destruction in March 1976. He asked the Rev. A. J. Finch to conduct the service. The opening prayers and Bible reading were read by the Rev. R. Haskins.

The contractor, Bro. D. L. McAvoy, a member of the lodge, handed Bro. Joe Davison the keys to perform the opening ceremony. Bro. Davison, a member of the lodge, donated the additional land necessary for the rebuilding of the hall. He was also an eyewitness to the explosion. Bro. Richard Jordan made a presentation to Bro. Davison on behalf of the officers and members of LOL 107. The Rev. A. J. Finch then said a prayer of dedication. A collection was taken up for the Building Fund and a buffet supper was provided in the new hall for all who attended.

Sir Edward Wingfield Verner's True Blues unfurled their banner on Friday 8 July 1977. Mrs Anna Haire unfurled the banner, which was donated to the lodge by her brother, Bro. George Duke, in memory of his father, Bro. Richard Duke, who was secretary for 47 years. The previous banner was destroyed in the terrorist attack the year before.

The platform party included the Worshipful District Master, Bro. H. Whitten, the District Secretary, Bro. W. D. Thompson, Bro. Rev. A. J. Finch, Bro. J. H. McCusker MP, Bro. John Toal, WM LOL 18, and Bro. Bob Blair, WM LOL 61. The Rev. D. Wilson of Knocknamuckley Parish Church said the opening prayers. Miss Linda Davison presented Mrs Haire with a pair of scissors to perform the unfurling and the Rev. A. J. Finch said dedicatory prayers. The lodge, headed by Edgarstown Accordion Band paraded a short way along the road and back to the church where tea was provided by members wives.

The previous banner was unfurled on 1 July 1965 by Bro. Leonard Wilson, the oldest member, at 8.00 p.m. at Knocknamuckley Parish Church. The lodge met at the hall at 7.30 p.m. and led by Bleary Pipe Band paraded to the church. Tea was afterwards served in the Parochial Hall. This banner was destroyed in the terrorist attack.

A banner was unfurled on 1 July 1939 at Knocknamuckley Parish Church by Bro. John Best, who was the oldest member of the lodge. The day previous a photograph was taken by Moffett's Studio at the church to commemorate the event. When the hall was attacked in 1976 this banner escaped serious damage and was carried at the Twelfth demonstration in Lurgan that year.

Ballygargan Orange Hall was destroyed in a terrorist attack on 28 March 1976. On the morning of 28 March the Worshipful Master, Bro. Eric Davison, received a phone message from the police, asking him to open Ballygargan Orange Hall to enable the army to make a routine check. He arrived about 11.00 a.m., opened the door, went through the main hall and into the kitchen with the soldiers. On returning to the main hall there was an explosion and he was thrown across the room. The trapdoor to the roof space was booby trapped and one soldier, Corporal Donald Traynor, was killed. The lodge lost a lot of artefacts, including photographs, furniture and banners. Upon reaching the road the Worshipful Master was informed that the police had received a message on the confidential phone saying arms were being stored in the hall. A floral tribute and letter of sympathy was sent to the family of the dead soldier. On 11 April a retiring offering was taken up in the three local churches – Knocknamuckley Parish Church, Bluestone Methodist Church and Newmills Presbyterian Church. The lodge met in the Victory Hall, Drumnacanvey, kindly loaned by Carrickblacker Guiding Star RBP 503, until the new hall was built.

LOL 107 is another of the major drumming lodges within the District.

Worshipful Masters 1935–1995:

1923–35	Bro. John Porter
1936–41	Bro. Richard Duke
1942–43	Bro. Joseph Livingstone
1944–45	Bro. James Davison
1946–48	Bro. Robert Davison
1949	Bro. Ernest Dickson
1950	Bro. James Adair
1951–83	Bro. Eric Davison
1984–86	Bro. George Wilson
1987–89	Bro. John Moffett
1990–92	Bro. Nigel Davison
1993–	Bro. John Gillespie

LOL 127 King William's Defenders, Portadown

The warrant No. 127 originally sat in Tandragee District. In 1795 the warrant was granted to James Quinn of Mullahead and the lodge was still sitting at this location by 1832. The year 1856 shows the Master as Thomas McKinney and a duplicate warrant in County Londonderry. The warrant No. 127 was to move to Portadown in 1890 where it took as its meeting place Parkmount. The lodge moved to Carleton Street Orange Hall when the new portion was built to the hall. The lodge became known as King William's Defenders in June 1900 and previous to this it had been called Verner's Golden Star. No. 127 is one of those lodges within Portadown District which has become synonymous with the area in which it once sat. It is often referred to as 'Parkmount' or 'The Walk' lodge.

Edward McCann was the Master of the lodge up to 1912 and in the early 1920s membership of the lodge numbered seventy. No meetings were held by the lodge from 1914 to 5 July 1918 due to the Great War and the large number of brethren who were away from home on active service with the forces. The Master reopened the lodge on 5 July 1918 as a number of disabled brethren had returned home and wished the lodge to be active again.

During World War Two Bro. David Gillis, who was serving with the Royal Air Force, was Killed In Action over Germany on 22 June 1940.

On 8 July 1955 the lodge unfurled a new banner featuring a portrait of King William III and a depiction of the *Mountjoy* breaking the boom. The ceremony was performed by the County Grand Master Wor. Bro. R. J. Magowan JP, OBE.

The Rt. Hon. William Craig MP, a member of LOL 291, was the special guest at the election of officers of the lodge in 1970. At the meeting Bro. T. Corkin was presented with a fifty-year service medal.

In 1990, as part of the celebrations to mark the tercentenary of the Battle of the Boyne, the brethren of LOL 127 were accompanied on parade by a goat. Parkmount Junior LOL 150 accompany the senior lodge on parade.

LOL 127 meets in Carleton Street Orange Hall although the lodge retains close links with the Parkmount area of Portadown. Castle Avenue in the Parkmount area was the natural choice as a venue for the unfurling and dedication of the lodge's new banner. The proceedings got under way at 8.00 p.m. on Friday 10 May 1991, with W. Bro. Harold Gracey, District Master acting as chairman and W. Bro. Reverend Tom Taylor leading the service. The unfurling of the banner, which features a portrait of King William III on the front and a representation of the *Mountjoy* breaking the boom, on the reverse was performed by Mrs Jennifer McCusker, the widow of the late Bro. Harold McCusker. Guest speakers on the evening included the County Grand Master, Right W. Bro. Norman Hood and Bro. David Trimble MP.

Three of the present members of the lodge hold fifty-year service medals, namely Bros. S. Thompson, W. Duke and W. Kerr.

Worshipful Masters of the lodge since 1934 are as follows:

1934–39	R. Ross
1940–58	H. Todd

1959	T. Austin
1960–70	W. Anderson
1971–73	T. Milligan
1974–75	C. Mathers
1976–77	T. Milligan jnr.
1978–79	J. Pickering
1980–81	R. Ramsey
1982–83	S. Thompson
1984–86	J. Uprichard
1987–88	W. Kerr
1989–90	T. Megarry
1990–	E. Lappin

Bro. Stanley Thompson, the current District Treasurer, is a member of this lodge.

LOL 161 Wesleyan Temperance, Portadown

Warrant No. 161 was established in Loughgall District in 1798 with James Sloan as Master. In early demonstrations LOL 161 carried a silk flag, bearing the Royal Coat of Arms, which had been originally presented to Lt.-Col. Robert Camden Cope and his troop of Volunteers in 1782 by the colonel's daughter.

In 1856 it was still at Loughgall with Jas. Woods as Master. The warrant fell dormant for a period of thirty years before coming to Portadown District in 1933. The lodge was opened by James Dermott, Portadown District Secretary, and David Rock, Asst. District Secretary, on Monday 6 March 1933. The first Worshipful Master of the lodge was Thomas Caddell. The lodge took as its title Portadown True Blues.

From its inception again in 1950, Wesleyan Temperance has had a strong Methodist membership. It was mainly members of that denomination who re-started the lodge.

For the past forty-five years Wesleyan Temperance LOL No. 161 has played a leading and influential part in the affairs of Portadown District LOL No. 1

The lodge banner for some thirty years had on one side a portrait of John Wesley, founder of Methodism. It had provided 161 with a unique and immediately recognisible place in the Portadown Orange parade.

Incidently, the portrait of John Wesley which adorned the 161 banneer for many years is now framed and much admired in the lecture hall of Thomas Street Methodist Church.

The 1950s was a great era for 161 as the membership soared above the sixty mark and at one time up to a dozen new members were being enrolled at some meetings. There were no fewer than seven Methodist ministers who were members of 161 at one time. At present there is one minister belonging to the lodge – the much-loved and respected Bro. The Reverend T. Henry Holloway, a past Worshipful Master of the lodge, and Portadown District Chaplain for many years.

Those 1950s' and '60s' demonstrations were memorable affairs as the lodge paraded behind Thomas Street Old Boys Silver Band.

Changing circumstances, not least social conditions, meant a decline in numbers in the 1970s and early '80s, but there is a great loyalty and resilience on the part of 161 brethren and in recent years the lodge has been making its mark once again with numbers on the increase and several brethren making an impact at District lodge level.

A dinner in 1990 to celebrate the fortieth anniversary of the lodge being formed again proved a landmark and since then the fortunes of Wesleyan Temperance LOL No. 161 have taken an upturn. The Twelfth dinner – always a high point of lodge activity – was revived and the brethren and the band which accompanies them now has the use of the new Methodist halls for that purpose.

In the 1950s and '60s, men prominent in civic and business affairs who were members included names like Robert Williamson, a Mayor of Portadown, Councillor John George McCann, Victor Reavie – whose cafe in Thomas Street was the venue for the lodge Twelfth dinner – and Councillor Ernest Downey.

The name Wright has always been to the fore in 161 and at one time four brothers of that family were members – Bros. Dick Wright, still a very active member, Earl Wright, who played a leading role in trade union and civic affairs, and the late Bros. Eric and Jim Wright – Jim passed away in April 1995. The lodge also has brethren in its ranks who rendered outstanding service in local government and two of those were the late Bros. Ken Jones and Billy Robinson.

Names like Percy Church, Bertie Montgomery, Norman Lyttle, Bobby Bell, and many others are remembered with affection by the brethren of 161.

Fermanagh man Bro. Cyril Stevens, who settled in Portadown in 1946, was recently presented with his 50-year membership jewel. It was a unique occasion, as Bro. Stevens' son, Paul, was initiated into 161 on the same night.

Worshipful Masters of LOL 161 since its re-inception are as follows:

1952–53	Bro. R. J. Williamson
1954–55	Bro. J. G. McCann
1956–57	Bro. W. J. Lyttle
1958	Bro. V. J. Reavie
1959–60	Bro. R. Wright
1961–62	Bro. W. K. Logan
1963–64	Bro. W. J. P. Church
1965–66	Bro. N. A. Lyttle
1967–68	Bro. W. Robinson
1969–70	Bro. C. Richardson
1971–74	Bro. Rev. T. H. Holloway
1975–76	Bro. W. Bailie
1977–78	Bro. D. Laverty
1979–81	Bro. R. H. Bell
1982–86	Bro. W. Bailie
1987–88	Bro. B. Courtney
1989–90	Bro. D. Burrows
1991–92	Bro. W. McClean
1993–94	Bro. J. Leckey
1995–	Bro. J. G. Leckey jnr.

LOL 172 St Saviour's True Blues, Clonroot

In 1796 this lodge number was meeting at Canoneil with Master George Morrow. Before coming to Portadown District in 1848 the lodge was meeting at Artabracka in 1820 and Mullahead in 1832. Two years after coming into Portadown District the number fell dormant and remained so to 1854 when it was given to Daniel Chapman at Drumnahuncheon. By the following January the warrant was again dormant. In July 1869 the first mention is made of the lodge being known as St Saviour's True Blues and 1875 John Robert Logan of Portadown is noted as Master. The Rev C. K. Irwin (Jun.), a member of 172, was a Deputy Grand Chaplain of Ireland in 1872.

Clonroot Orange Hall was erected in 1884.

The lodge's current banner, featuring a portrait of the late Bro. James McBroom and a painting of St Saviour's, The Dobbin, was unfurled in 1964.

Lodge officers for 1995 are as follows:

Worshipful Master ... Dennis Dunlop
Deputy Master .... Ronnie Hewitt
Secretary .... Alastair Hobson
Treasurer .... Bert Pierson
Chaplain.................... Herb McBroom

Herb McBroom is the lodge's longest serving member, having been in the lodge over seventy years.

LOL 273 The Rising Sons of Portadown

In 1798 warrant No. 273 was issued to Hugh Watson, Castlecaulfield District, Co. Tyrone. As in common with many other warrants a duplicate was issued to John Morrison, Garvagh District, Co. Londonderry, in 1829. The Co. Tyrone warrant was cancelled in 1890 and on 30 May 1895 a duplicate was issued to Portadown District at Carleton Street Orange Hall with District Master William John Locke. This warrant was to fall dormant a few months later. In June 1902 LOL 540, sitting in Carleton Street Orange Hall and formed in 1899 exchanged their warrant for that of No. 273. They carried across with them the name Christian Volunteers. J. A. Haire was the Worshipful Master and G. Matchett was Deputy. This lodge continued to function until 1962 when the warrant became dormant.

After a period of seven years the dormant warrant No. 273 was reconstituted on 5 November 1969 under the name The Rising Sons of Portadown. The Master at the lodge's reconstitution was Bro. Robert Jones. Since its reconstitution LOL 273 has continued to sit at Carleton Street Orange Hall.

On Friday 25 June 1971 LOL 273 unfurled its banner at a service of Dedication in Carleton Street Orange Hall. The banner depicts the scene of the drowning of the Protestants in the River Bann in 1641. A painting depicting the Crown and Bible is on the reverse.

The Rising Sons of Portadown was the

first lodge in Portadown District to carry the Bible in a glass case when on parade. In August 1976 the lodge members opened their new lodge room in Carleton Street Orange Hall. The members had undertaken the task of renovating two store rooms at the rear of the building to make them into a lodge meeting room and kitchen. In 1991 the lodge had the honour, along with LOL 99, of heading the District Mini-Twelfth parade which commemorated the 350th Anniversary of the 1641 massacre at the River Bann.

The Rising Sons of Portadown LOL 273 celebrated their 25th Anniversary in 1994.

Worshipful Masters of The Rising Sons of Portadown LOL 273:

1969–71	Robert Jones
1972–73	Samuel Anderson
1974–75	William Hanna
1976–77	W. J. McKinney
1978–79	James McKinley
1980–81	William Orr
1982–83	Cecil McVitty
1984–85	Robert Stewart
1986–87	Edward Jones
1988–89	William Power snr.
1990–91	Storey McIvor
1992	R. David Jones
1993–94	Kenneth Hobson
1995–	William Power jnr.

LOL 322 R. J. Magowan Memorial Temperance, Edenderry

The earliest recorded mention of warrant number 322 is found in the 1798 Minute Book of the Grand Orange Lodge of Ireland, but no other information is given. In 1829 the lodge was listed as working in Ballyronan, County Londonderry with William Banks as Worshipful Master. By 1856 a duplicate warrant had been issued to a lodge in Moneymore District. This lodge operated until 1890 when the warrant was returned to Grand Lodge. The Ballyronan lodge operated until 1931 when it became dormant.

On 30 May 1895 a further duplicate warrant was issued to Bro. John Black of Portadown on the formation of Lord Arthur Hill's LOL 322 sitting in Carleton Street Orange Hall (Arthur Hill was the late Unionist MP for West Down). This lodge functioned until

1905 when the members decided to merge with Dr Kane's Crimson Star LOL 417.

The inaugural meeting of Edenderry Temperance and Benefit LOL 322 was held on 13 May 1907 at Carleton Street Orange Hall with Bro. David Bright being installed as the lodge's first Worshipful Master a position he held until 1913. The lodge's first banner was unfurled in 1909 and featured King William III on the front and the Biblical 'Good Samaritan' scene on the reverse. This scene has been depicted on all the lodge's banners ever since. The cost of the banner was £13.

During the Great War many brethren served in the forces including W. J. Adair, Thomas Stewart, Thomas Hyde, James Chambers, Sandy Orr, David Boyd, James Johnston, William McClatchy, David Medlow, Robert Callison and James Gilliland. Bros. Chambers and Johnston were serving with the 36th (Ulster) Division and were wounded at the Battle of the Somme.

The foundation stone for Edenderry Orange Hall was laid by Mrs W. H. McCammon on 20 April 1920 and on 19 September 1925 the hall was officially opened. Prior to this date the brethren had met in Edenderry Parochial Hall. In 1936 a new banner featuring a portrait of Lord Carson was unfurled by Sister Mrs Magowan, the wife of Bro. R. J. Magowan, the long time Worshipful Master of LOL 322. The cost was £25.

The Second World War saw many Edenderry men again volunteering for service namely Joseph Gibson, Walter Curry, Gardiner Atkinson, Charles Johnstone, William Hewitt, Frank Radbone, Henry Kane and Frank Magowan, the son of R. J. Magowan. Bro. Kane was lost at sea on 21 June 1940 when his ship was torpedoed by a German U-boat.

In 1947 Bro. R. J. Magowan was elected as the first Mayor of the Borough of Portadown and two years later he received the OBE in the King's Birthday Honour's List. A new banner, the lodge's third, was unfurled in 1955, once again the ceremony was performed by Sister Mrs Magowan with Dr George Dougan presiding. March 1968 saw the end of an era with the death of R. J. Magowan, Worshipful Master of LOL 322 since 1934 and the District Master of Porta-down since 1955. The lodge was renamed the R. J. Magowan Memorial Temperance LOL 322 in memory of the late Worshipful Master and a new banner bearing this name was unfurled on 12 July 1971.

In 1982 Bro. John Brownlee became the second member of LOL 322 to serve as WDM of Portadown District. A member of LOL 322 for fifty years, Bro. Brownlee died in 1995.

The Reverend Tom Taylor dedicated a set of new officers' collarettes on 7 June 1995.

Since the death of R. J. Magowan the lodge's Worshipful Masters have been as follows:

1968–71	W. E. P. Hewitt
1971–73	Albert Greenaway
1973–75	W. S. McCauley
1975–77	David Allen
1977–79	T. R. Guy
1979–81	T. J. Dunn
1981–83	Noel McMurray
1983–85	Roy Jones
1985–87	Richard Morrison
1987–89	Martin Black
1989–91	James Edgar
1991–93	Eric Treanor
1993–95	John J. R. Mathers
1995–	James S. Kane

LOL 339 Corcrain Purple Rocket

This warrant first came to Portadown District in 1897. The warrant was in Omagh in 1829 and registered to a William Kerr in Omagh in 1891. In 1897 it was taken out in Portadown to replace No. 533. LOL 533 had been opened on 14 May 1894 by William J. Locke, District Master. It was decided at this meeting that the title of the lodge would be Corcrain Purple Rocket LOL. The word Temperance was not introduced to the following meeting. The first Master of LOL 339 was John Anderson. Erected as a memorial to the Late Bro. W. J. Locke, District Master of Portadown, Corcrain Orange Hall was opened by Mrs C. Johnston on 4 November 1911.

A number of memorial plaques have been erected in the hall in memory of past members of the lodge. On 30 June 1956 a memorial plaque was erected in memory of the Late Bro. John Wright for services rendered to the extension of the hall. Another was erected in memory of the Late Bro. Thomas Uprichard for services rendered to the hall and lodge from 1923–79. A plaque of Past Masters of the lodge was presented by the Milligan family in memory of the Late Bro. Cecil Milligan a member of the lodge for forty-six years who held the offices of Treasurer 1983–84 and Deputy Master 1985–86.

The members of the lodge unfurled their present banner featuring paintings of King William leaving Belfast Castle and the Biblical scene 'My Faith looks up to Thee' in 1977. The old banner was donated to a lodge in County Monaghan.

Throughout the period of the 'Troubles' Corcrain Orange Hall has been subjected to countless attacks by republicans. The hall has been daubed with paint and slogans, attempts have been made to set the hall on fire and cars belonging to members have been tampered with. No other Orange hall in Portadown has been on the receiving end of so many wanton and sectarian attacks. From 1985 there have been four arson attacks on the hall. A serious attempt to cause damage took place on 11 June 1994 when a security grill was broken off a window and a fire started in the Gents' toilets.

Corcrain LOL 339 held a special service on 15 May 1994 to commemorate the 100th Anniversary of the formation of the lodge. Over 300 members of Portadown District accompanied by Portadown Defenders Flute Band and Star of David Accordion Band attended a church service at Drumcree Parish Church. The dignitaries present included the County Grand Master, Bro. Norman Hood. The service was conducted by the Reverend John Pickering and the sermon was delivered by Reverend Bro. Tom Taylor, Deputy Grand Chaplain. In August 1995 Corcrain Orange Hall was seriously damaged in another sectarian attack.

Worshipful Masters of the lodge from 1913 are as follows:

1913–44	Thomas Boyle
1945–76	John Wright
1977–78	James Lutton
1979	Kenneth Love
1980–81	Robert Hughes

1982–83 Thomas Uprichard
1984–85 Alan Milligan
1986–87 David Rowan
1988–89 George Trouton
1990–91 Don Milligan
1992–93 Cecil Lutton
1994–95 Raymond Buckley

LOL 352 Derrykeevin Temperance

Warrant No. 352 came to Portadown District in 1896 when the officers and members of LOL 817 exchanged their warrant for LOL 352. LOL 352 was recorded in Lurgan District on 2 February 1829 and again in the Register for 1856.

LOL 817 was opened on 13 February 1886 by Rev. A. Leitch, District Master. It was known as Maiden City Fortress Temperance LOL. In 1825 LOL 817 was meeting at Derrylard with Richard Best as Master. In 1896 the Master of the LOL 352 was John Cooper who had also been Master of LOL 817. On 9 September 1898 the lodge minutes record that 'the office-bearers decided to keep their positions' but the minutes were left unsigned and sometime later warrant No. 352 was handed in. Warrant No. 352 was to be taken out again on 2 January 1933 when the name adopted was Derrykeevin Temperance LOL. The lodge was opened and the officers were installed by Major D. G. Shillington MP, District Master, Portadown District. The first Worshipful Master of the lodge was Bro. Joshua Crockett and he was followed by Jacob Benson who took over in 1934. Bro. Benson occupied the chair until 1980 when he was succeeded by Bro. Samuel G. Benson.

Members of the lodge erected an Orange hall in 1936 on land kindly donated by Thomas Trueman and within the hall is a plaque in memory of Thomas Trueman. The opening ceremony was performed by Lord Craigavon, the Prime Minister of Northern Ireland.

On 11 April 1950 the members of the lodge unfurled a new banner, featuring paintings of King William III crossing the Boyne and the 'Secret of England's Greatness'. This banner was painted by A. M. Purce & Co. Antrim at a cost of £80.

The lodge unfurled a new banner in June 1994. The ceremony was performed by Miss Hilda Trueman, the daughter of the late Thomas Trueman and the dedication was led by the Reverend Tom Taylor, Deputy Grand Chaplain. The new banner, painted by W. J. Jordan of Cookstown, cost £1,100 and features the same paintings as depicted on the previous one. After the unfurling ceremony the banner was paraded along a stretch of the Dungannon Road with Clonmacash Pipe Band providing the music.

The District Chaplain, Bro. George Robinson, is a member of this lodge.

LOL 371 Apprentice Boys, Drumnahuncheon

This warrant was first recorded in 1798 with William Hill as Master. By 1856 the number was in Lurgan District, sitting at Balteagh, with William Robinson as Master and in 1875 the position remains unchanged. With the coming of 1887 the warrant was recorded as in the hands of Richard Hobson and on 24 October of the same year the lodge was opened by the District Master, William J. Locke, at this meeting Richard Hobson was elected as Worshipful Master. The hall used by the lodge was opened in 1910 and in the early 1930s membership of the lodge was recorded at seventy.

Within the hall are two memorial tablets in honour of lodge members who served during the Great War and to those members who made the supreme sacrifice for King and Country. Those members who were Killed In Action were: A. Doherty, J. Courtney, A. Graham, T. Troughton, A. Loney, J. Taylor and J. Black.

In June 1936 the lodge unfurled a new banner, featuring a portrait of King William III on the front and a depiction of Saul sparing David's life on the reverse. The ceremony being performed by Bro. David Rock MBE, JP, County Grand Secretary. In 1964 a new banner, featuring a portrait of the late Bro. Richard Hobson and the Biblical scene 'No Cross No Crown', was unfurled in St Saviour's Church Hall by Mrs Lena Hobson.

The Dobbin Parish Hall was the venue for the unfurling and dedication of a new banner on 9 July 1993. The service was conducted by the Reverend E. T. Dundas and the unfurling ceremony was performed by Mrs June Pierson the wife of the Worshipful Master, Bro. William Pierson. A dedication was read by the Reverend Tom Taylor, Deputy Grand Chaplain. The banner features a portrait of the late Bro. Richard Hobson and a painting of the baptism of Jesus.

Bro. Tom Quinn, a Past Master of the lodge and one of the oldest Orangemen in the District, was presented with a Bicentenary Jewel by the District Master, Bro. Harold Gracey, at the annual Boyne Anniversary service at St Saviour's, The Dobbin, in 1995. Later members of LOL 371 presented Bro. Quinn with a special certificate marking his seventy-five years' membership of the lodge.

There is a strong tradition of Lambeg drumming within the lodge which has always been accompanied by drums on the 12 July. The last few years have seen a large influx of new young members into the lodge which augurs well for the future of the LOL 371.

Worshipful Masters of LOL 371 since 1935 are as follows:

1935–63	Richard Hobson
1964–72	Thomas Quinn
1973–75	James McClelland
1976–83	Robert Hobson
1984–94	William Pierson
1995–	Robert Hobson

LOL 395 Battlehill

No. 395 was taken out by the Master and members of No. 948 in 1895. The lodge was first known as Eldon LOL. Warrant No. 948 was initially established in 1796 at Magarity with the then Master Thomas Bradshaw. During the period 1823–1827 the lodge was meeting at Crowhill. By 1845 No. 948 was meeting at Cranagill but in 1850 the number had ceased meeting. On 6 October 1851 the warrant was handed to Alexander Trotter but on 7 June 1852 he lodged it with the District lodge. The following year in October 1853 the warrant was to be taken out again 'to be held in Corcullentrough' and by 1856 it was at Drumlellum before being returned, in 1857. In 1867 the warrant was working again and

in the late 1800s the lodge was meeting at Clonroot. James Hyde was Master in 1895 with the lodge meetings held in Mullan's house, Clonroot in an area known locally as Hivy Gap. When No. 948 finally ceased working in 1895 James Hyde became the Master of the new LOL 395.

When William J. Magee took over as Worshipful Master the lodge moved to the 'Walk' area of Battlehill and erected a tin hut in Kelly's field in which to hold meetings. This move was necessitated after Mullan's house in Clonroot was burned down with the loss of the lodge banner and one or two Lambeg drums.

The No. 395 was recorded in Co. Leitrim, at Manorhamilton District in 1856 with James Sharpe as its Master and by 1875 a duplicate was operating in Fermanagh. This duplicate would appear to have fallen dormant and in 1894 No. 395 at Manorhamilton had been cancelled.

A number of brethren from LOL 395 served during the Great War of whom four did not return, a Lambeg drum featuring a portrait of Lord Kitchener was dedicated by the lodge to their memory. Bro. Robert Devlin, who was later to occupy the deputy chair, served with the Royal Irish Fusiliers during the Great War and was wounded whilst serving in France. The lodge has a photograph of him in his army uniform and also retains his service medals.

In 1930 when Ballintaggart School House became vacant, members of the Mullholland family, whose relatives are still members of the lodge, spotted a local priest measuring up the site. Captain Lindsay of Hannavale House, another neighbour and Orangeman, became aware of this development and decided action was needed. He summoned Harry Grey WM of LOL 395 and Bob Devlin DM to a meeting and between them agreed to buy the school house for use as an Orange hall. Captain Lindsay kindly agreed to provide the necessary finance for the venture. The school house was bought from the Reverend Mr. Hogarth, Rector of St Saviour's, at the Dobbin, for the sum of £175.

A new banner for LOL 395 was unfurled on 12 July 1936, the ceremony was performed by Bro. Sam Mulholland with Bro. R. H. Bell presiding. The banner featured paintings of King William III crossing the Boyne and 'The Secret of England's Greatness'.

On Easter Monday 20 April 1981 the brethren of Portadown District assembled at Carleton Street and headed by the District Master, Bro. Herbert Whitten, paraded to Battlehill on the occasion of the re-opening of Battlehill Orange Hall.

The lodge's present banner was unfurled on 11 July 1987. The front features a portrait of the late Captain R. H. Lindsay of Hannavale House, who was instrumental in organising the purchase of Ballintaggart Old School House for use as Battlehill Orange Hall.

In 1994 two flags were presented to the lodge by Mrs Kathleen Power and her daughter Pearl, in memory of her late husband Bro. Joseph Power, Past Master of the lodge and late District Lecturer of Portadown.

The lodge has maintained its membership at around thirty-five with nine families: Patterson, Cooneys, England, Hewitt, Black, Hill, Wilkinson, Cahoun and Robinson making up the majority of lodge members.

Worshipful Masters of LOL 395 since 1935 are as follows:

1935–39	George Hewitt
1939–48	John McNeil
1949	James Tedford
1950	John Bell
1951	H. Magee
1952–58	Bertie England
1959	Bob Devlin
1960–72	Bertie England
1972–75	Sandy Hewitt
1977–78	Tom Black
1979–81	Robert Trimble
1982–84	Stephen Millar
1984–86	J. H. Power
1986	Carl Cunningham
1987–89	Robert Trimble
1989–94	J. H. Power
1995–	S. J. Power

LOL 417 Dr Kane's Crimson Star, Portadown

No. 417 first met at Ballinteggart in 1796 with Robert Kinney as Master. In 1823 the lodge was meeting at Mulladry but in 1850 it ceased working for a time. 1856 shows Daniel Magee as Master and the lodge sitting at Corcullentrabeg but by 1860 the warrant had been handed in again. In 1865 the lodge was again working at this time under the name of Tavanagh True Blues, Portadown, and John Leckey was Master. In 1875 a duplicate number was issued to John Wilson, Hollywood, Ballykeel. The year 1888 saw Portadown's LOL 417 called Ranfurly Royal Purple Banner with Robert Courtney as Master. In 1896 the lodge changed its name to Dr Kane's Crimson Star and in 1905 No. 417 amalgamated with No. 322 but retained the warrant No. 417.

LOL 417 unfurled their current banner on 20 May 1983. The ceremony was performed by the late Bro. Harold McCusker MP and the dedication performed by Bro. the Reverend Derek McMeekin. The front of the banner is adorned with the Bible and Crown, with the All-Seeing Eye, whilst the reverse pictures King William III crossing the Boyne.

An old photograph of the lodge was featured in the *Portadown Times* dated 25 November 1994. The photograph, which was taken in the early 1900s (possibly on the occasion of the unfurling of a new banner), shows lodge members together with their banner and two Lambeg drums. The banner featured in the photograph depicts a portrait of Dr Kane after whom the lodge was renamed in 1896.

Worshipful Masters of the lodge since 1934 are as follows:

1934–35	Matthew Redpath
1936–37	James Graham
1938–39	John George Blair
1939–41	William A. Black
1941–42	M. Magee
1942–43	A. Black
1943–45	Alexander Gill
1946–50	Ephraim Martin
1950–53	Thomas Mitchell
1953–60	William E. Burke
1960–62	Henry Wiggins
1963–76	William E. Burke
1977–79	Cecil Graham
1980–81	James Littlejohn
1982–83	Thomas Wright

1984–85	Reginald Tedford
1986–87	Joseph Watson
1988	James Tedford
1989–91	Garfield Tedford
1992–93	Robert Graham
1994–	Brian Doyle

LOL 417 meets in Carleton Street Orange Hall.

LOL 500 Harmony, Portadown

On 24 September 1828 this warrant is recorded in Monaghan, Co. Monaghan with Rev. H. L. St George as Master. In the Registry of 1856 the lodge was still at Monaghan with Master, Edward Smyth and in 1891 it was renewed to Joseph Lester Worshipful Master. The warrant was cancelled at the outbreak of the First World War in 1914. Warrant No. 500 came to Portadown District on 14 June 1944 when the warrant was taken out in the name of Joshua Ward, Worshipful Master. The lodge sat in Carleton Street Orange Hall.

Harmony LOL 500 became dormant in 1984.

LOL 608 Portadown Ex-Servicemen's

Warrant No. 608 is another of the warrants that came to Portadown from southern Ireland. On 4 November 1828 it is recorded at Ballymaehigh, Co. Cavan with William Byers as Master. By 1856 it was still in Co. Cavan this time at Ballyjamesduff with Thomas Hawthorn as Master. In 1875 the Master was recorded as Rev. Snegde Taylor and although the warrant was renewed in November 1897 it was to be cancelled on 17 December 1930.

Portadown Ex-Servicemen's lodge was formed on 14 February 1946 at a specially convened meeting of Portadown District LOL 1. Initially, the lodge took out warrant No. 413 but this was exchanged for warrant No. 608 in 1955. LOL 608 met for the first time under the new warrant on 8 September 1955. Since 8 September 1955 each meeting has begun with the Worshipful Master saying the Ex-Servicemen's Salutation followed by one minute's silence.

On 10 February 1956 a dinner was held to celebrate the tenth anniversary of the formation of the lodge.

In June 1961 the old standard, which featured Battle Honours of World War Two, was handed over to the County Grand Deputy Master, Bro. W. Gracey JP. Later that year Sir Norman Stronge was a guest of the lodge when he conducted the election of officers.

On 5 July 1962 a new standard, featuring the Battle Honours of World War Two was unfurled by the lodge. The chairman at the meeting was the WDM, Bro. R. J. Magowan OBE, JP.

On 11 April 1963 it was agreed by members of the lodge that members and former members of the Territorial Army and the Ulster Special Constabulary be allowed to join the lodge.

Bro. A. Rusk, a well-known personality in the town, joined the lodge in 1964 on transfer from LOL 99. A former sergeant in the Royal Artillery, Bro. Rusk served in France with the British Expeditionary Force where he was evacuated from Dunkirk in 1940. Later in the war Bro. Rusk took part in the Normandy landings, seeing service in France, Belgium, Holland and Germany.

In 1965 the late Bro. W. Cardwell joined the lodge on transfer from LOL 339. Bro. Cardwell had served with Lord Louis Mountbatten in South-East Asia and was a member of the Burma Star Association of which Lord Mountbatten was President. (A portrait of Lord Mountbatten is featured on the current standard of the lodge.)

Portadown Ex-Servicemen's LOL 608 has the honour of leading all parades of Portadown District LOL 1. This tradition began in 1969 when the lodge headed the Boyne Anniversary Church Parade to Drumcree. The following year the WDM, Bro. H. Whitten, again asked LOL 608 to lead the District church parade and also to lead the procession on 12 July.

Worshipful Masters of Portadown Ex-Servicemen's lodge are as follows:

1946–53	J. Walsh MM, JP
1954	Thomas Rea
1955	J. McKenna
1955–56	J. Heatley
1957	J. McKenna
1958–62	Thomas Mathers
1963	J. Allen

1964	T. Mathers
1965	A Hyde
1971–74	F. Dale
1975–76	D. Goddard MM, BEM
1978	G. Marsdon
1979–80	W. Cardwell
1981–83	A. Rusk
1984–85	W. Moffett
1986	C. Mathers
1987–88	R. Todd
1989–90	W. Totten
1991–92	E. Cleaver
1993	J. Best
1994	Brian Maguiness

LOL 608 has the eminent distinction of having provided no fewer than four mayors and one chairman of the two local government areas of Craigavon and Armagh. The mayors of Portadown who have been members of LOL 608 are Bro. Edward Cassells, Bro. Alfred Martin, Bro. Frank Dale and most recently Bro. Brian Maguiness who served as Mayor of Craigavon for the year 1994–95. In addition Bro. George McCartney was elected as chairman of Armagh District Council.

LOL 608 sits in Carleton Street Orange Hall.

XVI

The Orange Trail

A Guide for Visitors and Tourists

Now that we have read about the colourful and interesting history of Orangeism in Portadown District let us now take a closer look at some of the historical monuments, sites and locations linked with this glorious past. This is best achieved in the form of **The Orange Trail** an interesting and informative journey from the outskirts of Portadown to the very heart of the 'Hub of the North'. It is hoped that this trail will be of immense benefit not only to Orangemen from the Province but also to the many visitors and tourists from the rest of the United Kingdom and abroad that will visit the town during the summer months. It is expressly anticipated that many of those whose interest will have been whetted by reading this book will also take in the pageantry of the 12 July parades in all their colourful glory.

The trail begins at **Seagoe Orange Hall**, home of LOL 26, on a little laneway just off the Seagoe Road, near Seagoe Industrial Estate. Seagoe LOL 26 has a painting of Seagoe Parish Church depicted on its banner. This Orange hall was built in 1897 on land donated by Baroness Von Stieglitz, a member of the well-known Blacker family, which has featured prominently in this book. The Baroness also donated funds for the building of Carleton Street Orange Hall. Beside the hall is Seagoe Cemetery where the ruins of **Seagoe Old Church** are situated.

Within the ruins of this small church, lie the remains of many members of the **Blacker family** – most of whom were Orangemen. Although the headstones are now faded the names of many can still be discerned, including those of Major Stewart Blacker, Rev. Stewart Blacker, Rev George Blacker and the Rev James Blacker. There is unfortunately no headstone in memory of **Lt.-Col. William Blacker**, but the mortal remains of Portadown's most famous Orangeman lie with those of his family. William Blacker supplied much needed ammunition for, (courtesy of his father who at that time was re-roofing Carrickblacker House) and was present at the Battle of the Diamond which took place on 21 September 1795. After the battle plans got under way which led to the formation of the Orange Order. He took a keen interest in the development of the Orange Institution and became the first County Grand Master of Armagh.

This little church was rebuilt in 1660 by Valentine Blacker an ancestor of all the Blackers of Carrickblacker. The original church had been destroyed in the Irish Rebellion of 1641. A short walk away, within the cemetery itself and near the wall bounding the tennis courts, is the grave of **Samuel Giffin**, a young Portadown Orangeman who was killed at an anti-Home Rule rally in Dromore, County Tyrone in January 1884. A headstone was erected in his memory by the loyalists of County Tyrone. The cemetery also contains the burying ground of the Akinson family of Eden Villa in Bachelors' Walk. Wolsey Atkinson was the first treasurer of the Orange Institution and in 1797 became the Acting Grand Secretary of Grand Lodge.

Across the road on elevated ground stands the present **Seagoe Parish Church** built in 1814. Within the church are to be found many memorials to the Blacker family. Also of significant interest is the baptismal font which dates from the 1500s and which bears swordmarks inflicted by the rebels during the Irish Rebellion of 1641. An annual Orange service is held at this church on the Sunday before the 12 July.

Proceeding into the town via the Seagoe Road and Bridge Street you will pass **Edenderry Orange Hall**, home of

Edenderry LOL 322. This fine hall was constructed in 1924 and is the largest Orange hall within Portadown District (excepting Carleton Street). Continuing along Bridge Street we come to the impressive spans of **Edenderry Arch** (erected end of June to July each year) as part of the 12 July decorations. This arch dates from 1951 and is the largest arch in Portadown. Other arches that you may wish to visit during July are located at Jervis Street, Queen Street, Parkmount on the Garvaghy Road and at Margaret Street in Edgarstown. The arch in Margaret Street commemorates the Battle of the Somme which took place on 1 July 1916 in which 5,000 men of the 36th (Ulster) Division were killed or wounded. A must for all visitors is the unique Mournview Street arch which is one of the very few Black arches in Ulster. This arch was first erected in 1939, was put in storage during the war years and re-erected for the 12 July celebrations of 1945. For those wishing to see the traditional 'Eleventh' night bonfires pay a visit to any of the big housing estates in the town at Brownstown, Edgarstown or Killycomain. In Edenderry, however, an effigy of Lundy, the traitor who wished to surrender to the Jacobite forces at the siege of Derry in 1689, is traditionally consigned to the flames on the 1 July. The site of the bonfire is located at the bottom of Watson Street .

Further along Bridge Street is the present Bann Bridge widened in 1923. Turning left into the Pleasure Gardens and the Bowling Green we come to the location where in the **Irish Rebellion of 1641** hundreds of Protestant men, woman and children were drowned in the waters of the River Bann. There are many differing figures on the numbers of those killed but it is not less than 200. This event is depicted on the banners of two lodges within Portadown District. Watch out for them on the 12 July, they are: Johnston's Royal Standard LOL 99 and the Rising Sons of Portadown LOL 273. In those days the course of the river was slightly different flowing where the Bowling Green is now situated. On the 350th anniversary of this tragic event a simple religious service was held along the banks of the River Bann and a stone with

plaque commemorating the event was unveiled by the Right Honourable James Molyneaux MP.

Continuing our journey towards the town centre you will pass the site of **Burleigh House** where the present Meadow Lane is now located. Burleigh House was the home of Bro. John Burleigh the first District Master of Portadown from 1796 to 1807. Some Orange demonstrations were held within the grounds of this house. A few yards further up the town, near the present location of the Ulster Bank, stood **King William's Pear Tree**. Although King William never graced Portadown with his presence, units of his army were stationed there, including the king's own official cider maker! Across the road, in rooms above the Classic Bar, is where the world renowned painter, **Sir John Lavery**, sat whilst he painted his splendid canvas of 12 July, Portadown in 1928. The original is on display at the Ulster Museum, Stranmillis Road, Belfast – a visit to this award winning museum is highly recommended.

As we continue walking up the town you will see the magnificent clock tower of St Mark's Church, built to commemorate the men from Portadown who were killed in the Great War. Immediately in front of the church is the town's War Memorial and the imposing statue of **Colonel Edward James Saunderson**. The colonel who was born in 1837 and died in 1906 was MP for North Armagh and leader of the Irish Unionist Party as well as being a prominent Orangeman. He is famous for his rejection of the second Home Rule Bill by stating 'Home Rule may pass this House but it will never pass the Bridge at Portadown'. On a closer examination of the statue the colonel's foot can be seen trampling the Home Rule Bill. Each 12 July his statue is adorned with a traditional Orange sash. His portrait is depicted on the bannerette of Colonel Saunderson's Silver Stream LOL 58.

On the final leg of our journey we can see the **Central Markets** building where Portadown District Lodge met in the early days. Continuing along Church Street turn into **Carleton Street** which is the location of the Orange hall and the assembly point for the 1,200 members of the 32 lodges within

Portadown District on 12 July. **Carleton Street Orange Hall** was built in 1875, renovated in 1882 and refurbished in 1908 which is the date stone that can be seen on the facade. On 12 July morning this street reverberates to the sound of Lambeg drums, the skirl of the pipes and the shrill of the flute. Flags of all the nations in which the Orange Institution has a presence are displayed outside the Orange hall. For an experience of the sight and sounds of the traditional Ulster 12 July, Carleton Street is hard to beat.

This concludes our short but interesting tour of some of the sites linked with the Orange history of Portadown. We hope that you will enjoy this short introductory tour and that you make a point of visiting Portadown or the '**Orange Citadel**' on the 12 July to take in the carnival atmosphere of the Portadown Orange procession, a sight that moved Ulster's finest artist, Sir John Lavery, to record: 'I have seen many processions and exhibitions of intense feeling, but nothing to quite equal the austere passion of the Twelfth in Portadown'.

Appendix 1

District Masters of Portadown District LOL 1

1796–1807	John Burleigh	1854–1855	Thomas Dawson
1808 –1812	Richard Hunt	1856	Daniel Chapman
1812–1815	Henry Chamney	1856–1859	Robert Anderson
1816	Thomas Joyce	1860	John E. Brown
1817–1819	William Cregan	1861–1880	Robinson Ruddock
1820–1823	Curran Woodhouse	1881–1885	Joseph M'Caghey
1824–1825	Laurence Ruddock	1886–1891	Rev. Andrew Leitch
1826–1829	Daniel Bulla	1891–1905	W. J. Locke JP
1830–1835	John Hamilton	1905–1926	W. H. Wright
1836–1837	John Overend	1926–1944	Major D. G. Shillington. DL, MP
1838–1839	Rev. Charles King Irwin		
1844–1845	James Armstrong	1944–1955	Dr George Dougan DL, MP
1846–1849	Daniel Bulla	1955–1968	R. J. Magowan OBE, JP
1850	Rev. Henry de L. Willis	1968–1981	Herbert Whitten. JP, MP
1851	William Holland	1982–1985	John Brownlee.
1851–1853	James Searight	1986–	Harold Gracey

Appendix 2

Twelfth of July Venues Since 1870

1870	Carrickblacker	1914	Killylea
1871	Castledillon	1915	Moyallon
1872	Lurgan	1916	Cancelled as a mark of respect to the fallen of the Battle of the Somme.
1873	Armagh		
1874	Portadown	1917	Drumgor (Portadown and Lurgan Districts).
1875	Loughgall		
1876	Portadown	1918	Moyallon
1877	Killylea	1919	Carrickblacker
1878	Richhill	1920	Ballylisk (Opening of Orange Hall)
1879	Tandragee	1921	Loughgall
1880	Portadown	1922	Derryhale (Opening of Orange Hall)
1881	Killylea	1923	Newry (As a mark of respect for Protestants murdered at Altnaveigh the previous year)
1882	Lurgan		
1883	Carrickblacker		
1884	Newry	1924	Armagh
1885	Carrickblacker	1925	Richhill
1886	Portadown	1926	Tandragee
1887	Lurgan	1927	Portadown
1888	Portadown	1928	Lurgan
1889	Tandragee	1929	Bessbrook
1890	Dungannon Park	1930	Markethill
1891	Drumilly	1931	Killylea
1892	Richhill	1932	Drumbanagher
1893	Castledillon	1933	Keady
1894	Killylea	1934	Armagh
1895	Loughgall	1935	Portadown
1896	Portadown	1936	Richhill
1897	Lurgan	1937	Lurgan
1898	Portadown	1938	Tandragee
1899	Bessbrook	1939	Bessbrook
1900	Armagh	1940–44	No Celebrations took place due to Second World War.
1901	Tandragee		
1902	Lurgan	1945	Portadown
1903	Ashgrove (Portadown)	1946	Lurgan
1904	Loughgall	1947	Tandragee
1905	Richhill	1948	Poyntzpass
1906	Killylea	1949	Armagh
1907	Armagh	1950	Bessbrook
1908	Lurgan	1951	Portadown
1909	Portadown	1952	Lurgan
1910	Bessbrook	1953	Armagh
1911	Armagh	1954	Portadown
1912	Tandragee	1955	Lurgan
1913	Lurgan	1956	Tandragee

1957	Bessbrook	1976	Lurgan
1958	Armagh	1977	Killylea
1959	Markethill	1978	Keady
1960	Newtownhamilton	1979	Newtownhamilton
1961	Loughgall	1980	Markethill
		1981	Bessbrook

Policy adopted of selecting County venues
strictly by District number order.

1982	Portadown
1983	Richhill
1984	Loughgall

1962	Portadown	1985	Tandragee (Non-attendance by
1963	Richhill		Portadown District due to re-
1964	Keady		routing issue in Portadown).
1965	Lurgan	1986	Armagh
1966	Armagh	1987	Lurgan
1967	Tandragee	1988	Killylea
1968	Bessbrook	1989	Keady
1969	Markethill	1990	Newtownhamilton
1970	Newtownhamilton	1991	Markethill
1971	Portadown	1992	Bessbrook
1972	Richhill	1993	Portadown
1973	Loughgall	1994	Richhill
1974	Tandragee	1995	Loughgall
1975	Armagh	1996	Tandragee

Footnotes

Chapter I
1. Miller, David W., *Peep O' Day Boys and Defenders*, pp. 123–24.
2. *Ibid.*, p. 122.
3. Blacker, William and Wallace, Colonel., *The Formation of The Orange Order 1795–1798*, p. 30.
4. Miller, David W., *Peep O' Day Boys and Defenders*, p.124
5. Bardon, Jonathan., *A History of Ulster*, p. 204.
6. *Ibid.*, p. 175.
7. *Ibid.*, p. 205.
8. Blacker, William and Wallace, Colonel., *The Formation of The Orange Order 1795–1798*, p. 17
9. PRONI D1606/1/1/188
10. Wolsey, W. H., *Orangeism in Portadown District*, pp. 2–3.
11. Blacker, William and Wallace, Colonel., *The Formation of The Orange Order 1795–1798*, p. 102.
12. *Ibid.*, p. 102.
13. *Ibid.*
14. Wolsey, W. H., *Orangeism in Portadown District*, p. 5.

Chapter II
1. Blacker, William and Wallace, Colonel., *The Formation of The Orange Order 1795–1798*, pp. 115–116.
2. *Ibid.*, p. 147.
3. *Ibid.*, p. 123.
4. Bardon, Jonathan., *A History of Ulster*, p. 237.
5. Select Committee on Orangeism 1835.
6. Bardon, Jonathan., *A History of Ulster*, p. 237.

Chapter III
1. Wolsey, W. H., *Orangeism in Portadown District*, p. 6.
2. *Ibid.*, p. 70.
3. *Ibid.*, p. 6.

4. *Ibid.*
5. *Ibid.*
6. *Ibid.*
7. *Ibid.*, p. 13.
8. *Ibid.*, pp. 6–7
9. *Ibid.*, p. 7.
10. *Ibid.*
11. *Ibid.*

Chapter IV
1. Letter from Lord Gosford to Edward Lucas, 14 July 1845.
2. Wolsey, W. H., *Orangeism in Portadown District*, p. 7.
3. *Ibid.*, p. 7.
4. *Ibid.*, p. 9.
5. *Ibid.*
6. *Ibid.*
7. *Ibid.*
8. *Ibid.*, p. 10.
9. Sibbett, R. M., *Orangeism in Ireland and Throughout the Empire*, Vol. 2, p. 227.

Chapter V
1. Wolsey, W. H., *Orangeism in Portadown District*, p. 12.
2. *Ibid.*
3. *Ibid.*, p. 14.
4. *Ibid.*
5. *Ibid.*
6. *Ibid.*, p. 15.
7. McClelland, Aiken., *William Johnston of Ballykilbeg*, p. 25.
8. Wolsey, W. H., *Orangeism in Portadown District*, p. 15.
9. Sibbett, R. M., *Orangeism in Ireland and Throughout the Empire*, Vol. 2, p. 586.

Chapter VI
1. Wolsey, W. H., *Orangeism in Portadown District*, p. 18.
2. *Historic Monuments of Northern Ireland*, p. 86.
3. Bardon, Jonathan., *A History of Ulster*, p. 374.

Chapter VII

1. McConkey, Kenneth., Sir John Lavery, p. 162.

Chapter XII

1. Brendan McKenna had a conviction for the part he played in the bombing of the Royal British Legion premises at Thomas Street, Portadown, in the 1970s. Portadown District Officers had consistantly maintained that they would not take part in discussions with known convicted terrorists.

Bibliography and Sources

Bardon, Jonathan *A History of Ulster* The Blackstaff Press 1992

Blacker, Colonel William & Wallace, Colonel Robert H. *The Formation of the Orange Order 1795 - 1798* Edited Papers Education Committee The Grand Orange Lodge of Ireland 1994

County Armagh Grand Orange Lodge *Souvenir Booklet - The Story of the Battle of the Diamond* By W.H. Wolsey, Loughgall 12 July 1961

County Armagh Grand Orange Lodge *Official Brochure of the 292nd Anniversary of the Battle of the Boyne,* Portadown 12 July 1982

County Armagh Grand Orange Lodge *Official Brochure of the 303rd Anniversary of the Battle of the Boyne,* Portadown 12 July 1993

Jones, R. David *A History of LOL 273* Unpublished Booklet

Kane, James S. *A History of Edenderry LOL 322* Unpublished Booklet

Kane, James S. *For God and the King – The Blackers of Carrickblacker* Ulster Society (Publications) Ltd., 1995

McClelland, Aiken *William Johnston of Ballykilbeg* Ulster Society (Publications) Ltd 1990

McConkey, Kenneth *Sir John Lavery* Canongate Press Edinburgh 1993

Miller, David W. (Ed.) *Peep O'Day Boys and Defenders* PRONI, Belfast 1990

Sibbett, R.M. *Orangeism In Ireland and Throughout the Empire* Vols 1 &2 Thynne & Co. Ltd 1938

Wolsey, W.H. *Orangeism In Portadown District* Portadown Times 1935

Journals, Magazines and Newspapers
Armagh Guardian
Belfast News Letter
Belfast Telegraph
Irish News
Newry Telegraph
New Ulster - The Journal of the Ulster Society
Orange Standard
Portadown News
Portadown Times
Seagoe Church Magazine

Minute Books
Minute Books of The Grand Orange Lodge of Ireland
Minute Books of Portadown District LOL 1
Minute Books of Private Lodges in Portadown District LOL 1
Registers of The Grand Orange Lodge of Ireland